Gertrude Blom

Bearing Witness

Gertrude Blom
Bearing Witness

Edited by Alex Harris and Margaret Sartor

Published for The Center for Documentary Photography,

Duke University, by The University of North Carolina Press

Chapel Hill and London

Photographs
© 1984 Gertrude Duby Blom

"Introduction" by Alex Harris, "Tzotzil
and Tzeltal: Who in the World?" by Robert
M. Laughlin, and "The Lacandones,
Gertrude Blom, and the Selva Lacandona"
by James D. Nations © 1984 The Center
for Documentary Photography, Duke
University

Manufactured in the United States
of America

Library of Congress Cataloging in
Publication Data

Blom, Gertrude Duby.
  Gertrude Blom—bearing witness.

  1. Photography, Documentary. 2. Mayas.
3. Blom, Gertrude Duby, 1901– . I. Harris,
Alex, 1949– . II. Sartor, Margaret, 1959– .
III. Title.
TR820.5.B59 1984   770'.92'4 [B]   83-23272
ISBN 0-8078-1597-7

Lines from "The Guardian,"
by Mark Strand, in *Selected Poems*
(Atheneum Publishers, 1980).
The editors gratefully acknowledge the
permission of the author to reprint this
poem.

Photograph by Teobert Maler, Courtesy
Peabody Museum, Harvard University,
copyright © President and Fellows of Harvard College 1983. All rights reserved.

Designed by Richard Hendel

Set by The University of North
Carolina Press in Eric Gill's Joanna type

Printed by Meriden Gravure Company
on Lustro Offset Enamel

Bound by Kingsport Press

The jaguar logo used throughout the book
is the symbol for Na Bolom, Gertrude
Blom's home in San Cristóbal de las Casas,
Mexico. It is a copy of a jaguar from a frieze
on a building at the ruins of Tula in the
Mexican state of Hidalgo.

To the memory of
Bartolomé de Las Casas,
1474–1566

Contents

Acknowledgments

Gertrude Blom—Bearing Witness and the concurrent exhibition tour of Blom's photographs are the result of two and a half years of work involving many people. The editors are particularly indebted to the staff and volunteers at Na Bolom, the Center for Scientific Studies that is also Gertrude Blom's home in San Cristóbal de las Casas, Mexico. From Na Bolom, we wish to thank individually Ken Nelson, Berthalicia Rivas, Joan Darby Norris, and Barry Norris. In 1982, Barry came to the United States to make all the prints for the book and exhibition, an achievement that speaks for itself.

Many of the photographs in the book and exhibition were chosen from a portion of Blom's archive that was not previously accessible. In the early stages of the project, amid the ash fall from the eruption of El Chichonal, Tim Burns traveled to Na Bolom and worked for three months to make contact prints of over six thousand of these negatives.

The editors are grateful for the hard work and guidance of the staff of the University of North Carolina Press, and want to thank especially Richard Hendel, Iris Hill, David Perry, and John Rollins.

At the International Center of Photography in New York, we have worked closely with Cornell Capa, William Ewing, Willis Hartshorn, Art Presson, and Steve Rooney to plan the exhibition of Gertrude Blom's photographs. This is the second in a series of exhibitions and symposiums on photography in the humanities organized jointly by the Center for Documentary Photography and the International Center of Photography. For its support of both these projects, we gratefully acknowledge the National Endowment for the Humanities, a federal agency.

We wish to thank Martha Cappelletti and the staff of the Smithsonian Institution Traveling Exhibition Service for their help in sponsoring the exhibition tour of Gertrude Blom's photographs, "People of the Forest." Institutions participating in the tour to date are the Chicago Academy of Sciences, the Princeton University Library, Duke University, the Institute of Latin American studies at the University of Texas, and the Peabody Museum at Harvard University.

The following people have also contributed in diverse ways to this project: Alfred Bush, Robert Bruce, John Cotter, William deBuys, Peter Decker, Peter Filene, Gary Gossen, Nick Kotz, Robert Laughlin, Patsy McFarland, Walter Morris, Edward Ranney, Carol Shloss, Evon Vogt, Robert Wasserstrom, and Carter Wilson. We want to thank as well Herbert and Betty Morse, deeply committed environmentalists, for their generous support of this volume. For help and advice throughout the work on this book and exhibition, we have relied particularly on James Nations.

This book and the other books and programs of the Center for Documentary Photography exist primarily through the generosity of the Lyndhurst Foundation. Alex Harris would like to thank Bruce Payne, Joel Fleishman, Robert Behn, and his other colleagues at the Institute of Policy Sciences and Public Affairs at Duke University for their support of his work at the center. As in previous projects, the advice and encouragement of Robert Coles has been essential to the publication of this book.

Gertrude Blom

Bearing Witness

The sun setting. The lawns on fire.
The lost day, the lost light.
Why do I love what fades?

You who left, who were leaving,
what dark rooms do you inhabit?
Guardian of my death,

preserve my absence. I am alive.

Mark Strand

1951 Lacanjá Chan Sayab, Trudi and Maria in Lacandon milpa

Introduction

Alex Harris

Of all the qualities needed by a social observer photographer—from a high degree of motivation and an eye for the essential to a keen sense of light, composition, and timing—perhaps the most important is a quality called in Mexico "*el don de gente*," or "a way with people." A physician might use this same manner to gain the trust of a patient, a politician would find such charisma necessary to get elected, a priest or rabbi would need a similar genius to truly inspire his congregation. This "don de gente" is not a science and cannot be taught. For those who have it, as for Gertrude Duby Blom, it is a gift that comes naturally, from within.

Over the past forty years, traveling throughout the highland forests and lowland jungles of Chiapas, Mexico, Blom has been uniquely situated to make a powerful and revealing portrait of the Ladino and Mayan peoples of that state. She has lived beside and photographed the highland Maya, the same Tzotzil and Tzeltal Indians evoked in Robert Laughlin's accompanying essay. Indeed, almost half the photographs reproduced here are devoted to Blom's work among the highland peoples. But of the nine distinct groups of Maya she has photographed in Chiapas, Blom has been especially attached to one small group, the Lacandon Maya, who inhabit the lowland jungle that borders Guatemala, to the east of her home in the town of San Cristóbal de las Casas.

It is particularly in her photographs of the Lacandones and their jungle environment that Gertrude Blom joins the ranks of other great social observers with a camera, like Laura Gilpin, Dorothea Lange, and Eugene Smith,

photographers who earned the trust of their subjects, in part, because they cared a great deal for the lives and fates of the people they portrayed. What separates Blom from these photographers, and makes her extensive body of work seem particularly impressive, is that for her, photography is not a primary concern. Blom's photographs are a by-product of her many other activities over the years. In Mexico she is part journalist, social activist, and explorer, part anthropologist, photographer, and ecologist, and, it would not be an exaggeration to state, part legend.

In July 1982, when Margaret Sartor and I traveled to Gertrude Blom's home in San Cristóbal de las Casas, we knew she had been an antifascist organizer in the Weimar Republic of Germany and we had heard about her fight to save the last great rainforest of southern Mexico. But what brought us to this remarkable Spanish colonial town in the mountains at the southern tip of Mexico was a photograph.

The year before, at the International Center of Photography in New York, I had seen a picture Blom made in 1959 of a young Lacandon boy huddled in the bow of a dugout canoe. The picture radiated a haunting presence. The immense silence of the lake and the fragile sadness of the boy's expression remained with me. Curiously, I would remember this experience not as a photograph seen but as a moment lived; as if in a dream I felt I had been to that northern Lacandon settlement and recalled the feeling of that day on Lake Najá.

In order to meet Gertrude Blom and find out more about her work, I made my first short trip to

4

Mexico in March of 1982. During that week I reviewed enough of Blom's extensive photographic archive to decide to publish a book devoted to her work as a photographer. At that point, I intended, in true academic fashion, to introduce her pictures with an essay about photography, noting Blom's reflections on the artistic value of this or that image, with perhaps a thought or two on the symbolic significance of her work. But that essay was not to be written.

Over the next two summers, Margaret and I worked together to edit Blom's photographs, and to conduct a series of interviews with Blom about her life and work. We learned soon enough that she was unwilling to talk about her photographs as objects or works of art. She would not generalize about photography or in any way give us an intellectual explanation of how she worked with a camera. If we showed her a photograph that for us was particularly moving, she would always talk about the person or the place, the day or expedition to the jungle, but never about the photograph. As the boy in the dugout canoe had become for me, these were specific moments she had lived and people she had come to know.

On my first trip to Mexico, I had a long conversation with Gertrude Blom about her photographs. I had spent several days immersed in her photographic archive, and was just beginning to get a sense of the scope of her accomplishment. On the afternoon when I broached the subject of publishing a book of her work as a photographer, Blom stopped me in mid-sentence and said, with what seemed a mixture of pride and surprise, "But I am not a photographer!"

She is not alone in assuming that a photographer with a good eye must also have a fascination with the process of photography and a knowledge of the medium in order to be taken seriously as an artist. In the current mass of books and exhibitions many editors and curators continue to show their preference for photographers with increasingly sophisticated and arcane approaches to the medium. Accordingly, in its short history, whenever photography has looked cautiously over its shoulder at the other arts or held a narcissistic concern for the photographic process, the vitality of the world has been noticeably lacking from the work produced. One need only review the enormously significant body of work assembled by the French photographer Eugene Atget at the turn of the century, or consider Eudora Welty's simple and straightforward photographs of Mississippi during the Depression, or study the plates discovered recently of the small-town Arkansas portrait photographer Mike Disfarmer from the 1940s, to understand the virtues of remaining isolated and perhaps totally ignorant of the sophisticated battles being fought in the name of photography.

At the end of my first week in Mexico, on a drive down the mountain from San Cristóbal de las Casas to the state capital of Tuxtla Gutiérrez, Blom agreed to the publication of her photographic work as a book. Not wanting to conceal my enthusiasm for the project, I immediately mentioned certain extraordinary photographs from the portion of her archive I had looked through. These were pictures that I was sure would be included in the book. But my excitement that day

was not shared. In a subdued voice, Blom frankly expressed disappointment in her photographs, complaining that nothing ever came out the way she really saw it.

At the time, I assumed she was talking about her lack of technical expertise and her frustration at how much was lost between the seeing and the printing of her pictures. Months would pass before I really understood how wrong I had been in assessing her disappointment in photography.

One afternoon Margaret and I showed Blom a print of a recent portrait she had made of her closest living friend among the Lacandones, Chan K'in Viejo, the t'o'ohil, or "spiritual leader," of the northern Lacandones. After looking closely at the print for a moment she said, "I think I see too many different things in a person, and it never comes out that way on film. I always see more than the camera gives me."

I realized then why I had not been able to understand what Blom had been trying to tell me that day on our drive down the mountain. We had not been speaking the same language at all. The more "sophisticated" practitioner would never expect to find on a thin sheet of film all that Blom hopes to see there. She wishes to capture in a portrait not only what she sees but all that she feels about a person; hence she is always disappointed.

In choosing the photographs for this book, and the concurrent exhibition at the International Center of Photography, we had expected to work closely with the photographer. After all, we had the responsibility for selecting a tiny fraction of her work, about one hundred photographs, to represent the forty thousand black-

and-white pictures Blom had made since coming to Mexico in 1940. We were careful to choose photographs characteristic of the body of her work, but we looked for images with especially powerful visual and emotional impact. After a few weeks we were surprised and somewhat bewildered that Blom did not once suggest any changes in our selections, nor did she ever seem genuinely concerned with the day-to-day work on the book. We came to understand Blom's reticence was less an endorsement of our editorial judgment than the result of her attitude about her photographs. Unlike any other photographer we had ever met, Blom held most of her photographs in equal regard, viewing each picture as another small part of her experience in Chiapas.

Students of ethnology may at first be disturbed by the seemingly indiscriminate mix of culture and chronology in the sequencing of the photographs reproduced here. Indeed, as evident in the bibliography of this book, Blom's portraits have traditionally been used to good advantage in a more scholarly fashion than we have intended here. More often than not, her photographs have illustrated specific historical or anthropological themes, the images subordinate to and necessarily limited by the text they accompanied. In this book, however, we have tried, with what success others must judge, to realize the potential of Blom's pictures to communicate in a more universal and perhaps richer way, without being bound by the concerns of one or another discipline.

Photography, in and of itself, does not interest Gertrude Blom. She has never thought much

about the medium or studied the work of master photographers in order to improve her skills. When we mentioned to her the names of photographers important to the documentary tradition—August Sander, Laura Gilpin, and Walker Evans, among others—we found she knew little or nothing of their work.

Even more surprising for a woman who has continually used her camera for over forty years, Blom possesses no interest in the craft of photography, in developing her own negatives or perfecting the print-making process. She has always been able to find someone to produce her prints, and over the years has become more critical, and, it should be said, more and more fortunate, in her choice of printers.

Barry Norris, her printer and close friend since 1977, was already an accomplished photographer and master technician when he arrived in San Cristóbal and took over the organization of her photographic archive. With his help, her negatives have been printed to their full potential for the first time. Norris has also been a translator and, in many ways, an editor for Blom. She has come to trust and rely on his judgment, both in the selection of her photographs as well as in the way these images should be rendered. It is no coincidence that Blom's reputation as a photographer has soared in the years of her unique collaboration with Norris.

Blom has also come to know some of the prominent young Mexican and American photographers who travel to Chiapas each year. However, unlike a whole generation of contemporary photographers who flaunt only what is grotesque in people, Blom is in-

clined to show what is affirming. As many of us unconsciously edit the memories of our lives, particularly those of childhood, so that only the sweet ones linger in our minds, so Blom uses her camera to hold on to the beautiful things she has seen. Given the horrors of Nazi Germany she witnessed as a young woman, it should not be surprising to find this photographer seeking to validate the very best qualities of mankind. Blom's photographs of people document the existence of a better world, and, no less important, they confirm her ties to the Lacandones, a tribe representing the antithesis of all she left behind in Europe.

There has never been anything coy about Gertrude Blom's manner with people. She can at times be so forceful and direct as to disconcert the uninitiated visitor and intimidate anyone not determined to stand up to her. Yet this same manner has elicited the bold expressions to be found throughout her entire body of work. One can only conclude that with the Maya of Chiapas, Blom has met her match.

It would be easy to misinterpret the expressions one finds on these faces. What might be taken as arrogance by an intrepid American tourist or construed as the anger of the proletariat by any well-intentioned Marxist scholar is, quite simply, a quality of self-possession foreign to the experience of most Occidentals.

These are the four hundred Lacandones who call themselves the hach winik, or "true people," and, like their Tzotzil and Tzeltal neighbors in the Chiapas highlands, they consider their language the "true word." These 130,000 people of Chamula and Zinacantán have no doubt that their distinct ceremonial centers are the *smixik' balamil*, or "navel of the earth."

An outsider is always tempted to pity the Mayans wandering barefoot through the streets of San Cristóbal de las Casas or hoeing their milpas in the hills beyond the town—all dreadfully poor people by almost any western standards. If we take the time to look closely, however, and really see the expressions in those eyes that return our gaze, we will sense no small amount of sympathy directed at us—for all those without the protection of their saints, for all those outside of the tribe.

If we are to be justified in feeling compassion for the people of Chiapas, it should be to mourn the loss of their once great tropical rainforest, the home of the Lacandon Maya. Since 1960, in one of the indisputable tragedies of the twentieth century, over four million acres of this lowland jungle have been destroyed by slash-and-burn farmers, lumber companies, and cattle ranchers. Moreover, far from taking a neutral stance on the deforestation of Chiapas, the government of Mexico, troubled by overpopulation and, more recently, a huge foreign debt, has implemented policies that have hastened the destruction.

Over the last twenty years, Gertrude Blom has become more and more concerned, lately to the point of obsession, with this ongoing ecological disaster. Since 1970 she has practically abandoned photographing people in favor of documenting the destruction of the ancient trees.

When we began to look for a title for this book, one phrase or line to stand for Gertrude Blom's work with the camera, we came across an old Quaker term, "bear-ing witness." According to this fundamental tenet of the Quaker faith, if one is aware of an injustice, one has a responsibility to act accordingly, even if those actions are contrary to commonly held beliefs of society. To sit idly by in the face of something perceived as wrong is unacceptable. Blom uses her camera to bear witness to the unnatural destruction of her corner of the world, much in the way she worked against the rise of fascism in Europe before World War II, in protest against what she knows is wrong and must be rectified.

It is no small irony that this woman who for years has opposed the undermining of traditional Lacandon culture by fundamentalist Christian missionaries has herself taken on many of the characteristics of these fervent jungle preachers. Like the early Christians who felt compelled to go out into the world and, in another sense of the phrase, "bear witness" to the one true faith in hopes of making converts, so Gertrude Blom preaches her message to all who will listen—and to many who will not. Her religion is the trees that for years have sustained and protected the Lacandones, and her message—to stop the destruction.

As more and more of the jungle disappears, the message becomes more strident, and more difficult to ignore. In her old age, Blom has come to resemble the Old Testament prophet who cries, not in the wilderness, but for it; meanwhile, the pace of destruction quickens, with no end in sight.

As an important part of her crusade against the seemingly inevitable, Blom uses her camera in a manner that follows the central documentary tradition, as Jacob Riis and Lewis Hine used theirs earlier in this century: to provide evidence, indisputable visual proof, of an injustice. Like those earlier photographic crusaders, Blom is making propaganda, not in the prevailing negative sense of the word, but in a way closer to its original meaning in which a propagandist was one who spread the faith.

Looking at her photographs of the charred and burning forest, of huge tree trunks piled like corpses for mass burial, one is reminded of an earlier American documentary photographer, Mathew Brady, and his photographs of the aftermath of the great Civil War battles. In Brady's photographs, as in those by Blom, one can feel the brutal horror of what has just taken place and see all too clearly the tragic waste that should never be repeated.

One need only read the accompanying article by Gertrude Blom to understand the intensity with which she mourns the passing of the Lacandon jungle. In recent years she has come to share the apocalyptic vision that now preoccupies her old friend, Chan K'in Viejo, the great prophet of the northern Lacandon Maya. Chan K'in states unequivocally that the roots of all living things are tied together; when the Lacandon forest is destroyed and the last of the "true people" dies, the world will end.

In the sacred book of the Maya, called the Popol Vuh, one learns that humankind is currently in its third incarnation. Twice before the gods of the ancient Quiché Maya destroyed the men and women for ceasing to venerate their makers. Blom argues convincingly that we are well into another cycle of mass destruction. She sees the bitter irony of a modern age in which humankind, possessed by greed, hastens its own extinction.

In fighting to save the Lacandones and their jungle, Blom is working in a tradition that is over four centuries old, following quite literally in the footsteps of Fray Bartolomé de Las Casas, to whom this book is respectfully dedicated. Las Casas, the first bishop of Chiapas, was a man of action, determined to protect the Indians of the sixteenth century from the greed and abuse of the Spanish conquistadores. For fifty years of his long life, he battled, practically by himself, against the accepted Spanish system of *encomienda* and *repartimiento*, by which the Indians were virtually enslaved in return for the "protection" of the crown and religious instruction.

As a journalist, Blom has written hundreds of articles over the years condemning the policies that have caused irreparable harm to the land and people of Chiapas. Las Casas in his day was also a remarkably prolific writer. In order to gather information to prove to the crown that the sixteenth-century Indians should be treated fairly, Las Casas became a serious student of their languages and customs and wrote persuasively to disprove the generally accepted Aristotelian theory of the inferiority of certain classes of people. In his *Brief Account of the Devastation of the Indies*, first published in Seville in 1552, and his huge *History of the Indies*, written between 1527 and 1561, he detailed an eyewitness account of the genocide and horrifying abuses against these defenseless natives. As Blom would be later, Las Casas was an outspoken and stubborn fighter for social justice, and, like her, he had a concern for the protection of the nat-

ural environment. It is appropriate that in 1963 Blom was named the president of the Patronato Fray Bartolomé, an organization in Chiapas dedicated to research and publication in the spirit of this great bishop.

At eighty-two, Gertrude Blom is a woman of extremes and contradictions. Often the personal qualities that attract people to her can also drive them away. She is, above all, a born fighter with extraordinary energy and a relentless attack. She is a teacher, by example, without the patience one normally associates with that calling. She is the dignified matriarch and the spoiled child; the generous mentor who can, in a moment, seem cruel or insensitive. Blom is flamboyant, yet manages to live a simple life, and although the needs of her ego are huge, they are tempered by a penchant for self-criticism and a willingness to apologize. In the end one senses about her what the Lacandones have always said: that "her heart is good."

Several writers have attempted biographies of Gertrude Blom, and it is no wonder, given the drama of her life story. In gathering information for this book, we were given no more or less detail than any of these earlier interviewers. Blom is an intensely private person. In Mexico, however, she is also very much a public figure, and so she continues to be protective of her past history in the way any public figure might be. As we sat with Blom in her "cueva" listening to her stories, we had at times the feeling of being spoon-fed a legend, piece by piece. Later, trying to put those pieces together, we found many gaps in her account. The saga that emerges is clearly the one that Blom intends

us to know, but it is, quite probably, the only version anyone will ever have.

Europe

"Trudi" was born Gertrude Elizabeth Loertscher, in the canton of Berne, in the Swiss Alps, in 1901. A Protestant minister's daughter, the middle child with an older sister and younger brother, she grew up in the country village of Wimmis, where her father preached. Never an enthusiastic student, Trudi preferred the outdoors to the time she was forced to spend in the classroom. Perhaps her most pleasant memories of primary school years were the books written by an exceptionally popular German novelist, Carl May, who described the Indians of the Americas, though, in fact, he had never traveled far from Berlin. Like millions of other European children, Trudi would follow the exploits of May's virtuous Teutonic protagonist, Karl, as he fought both to save the Indians from greedy Yankees and to protect them from the perils of instant civilization. After school, on a beautiful mountain meadow with reeds and a small stream, Trudi would play "Indians" with her friends. Seventy years later, she still remembers not allowing anyone but herself to play the role of the Indian chief.

Trudi's most vivid memories of childhood foreshadow both her love of adventure and the courage she would need later in life. Like other young children, she was afraid of the dark, but by the age of five Trudi had devised a plan to get rid of her faintheartedness.

8

One day I decided this situation is impossible, that I could not be scared anymore. I forced myself to go to the graveyard in Wimmis at dusk, down by the church, down on the edge of the forest near the town. The first time I went halfway and ran back frightened to death. Every evening I went a little farther until I could go to the cemetery. I would imagine skeletons on my back and run home. Finally, I was able to stay, without fear, until it was dark, and walk calmly home to go to bed.

When she was still in primary school, Trudi's family moved away from Wimmis and the countryside she loved into the much larger town of Berne, first to a big house and later to an apartment building. In the apartment downstairs lived Herr Duby, the general secretary of the trade union for Swiss railway workers. It was he who introduced Trudi to socialist ideas. There was a boy in the family, Kurt, about her age, and they became fast friends. As the years passed and their friendship and involvement in socialist politics deepened, they married.

By the time she was sixteen, Trudi had adopted her own political ideas, and she and her politically conservative father began to quarrel a great deal.

In many ways my father and I were extremely alike—both fighters in a way and neither of us very tolerant of different opinions. Once I started to think for myself, I became the black sheep of the family and we didn't get along very well anymore. In fact, I left home at quite a young age.

The next year, in the town of Niederlenz, Trudi enrolled in a two-year horticulture program, from which she would earn a degree. In 1918, in the middle of the academic year, there was a general strike in Switzerland; all

the schools closed, and Trudi returned to Berne.

Against her parents' wishes, she and Kurt Duby went into town and sat in on many heated sessions of parliament. They heard arguments for and against the eight-hour work day and witnessed the fistfights that sometimes broke out between opposing legislators. A controversy raged in parliament over the government's refusal to allow for the celebration of the Russian Revolution, one of the causes of the general strike. Back in horticulture school, she began to meet regularly with other students for political discussion.

Trudi became even more involved in politics at the school for social work she attended two years later in Zurich. She tells of having tremendous energy as a young woman, many times staying up all night to work for the socialist youth movement she helped to start in Zurich.

She began to contact the socialist papers in Switzerland, the *Tagwacht* in Berne and the *Volksrecht* in Zurich, in hopes of writing articles for them. This was the beginning of a working relationship with these papers that was to last through Hitler's rise in Germany. At the age of twenty-three, when she left home to travel, Trudi took on the role of self-appointed correspondent for the Swiss papers, reporting on the socialist movement in other parts of Europe.

In England, Trudi lived for a year as a volunteer in the home of a Quaker family. She became good friends with Henry Noel Brailsford, the editor of the *New Leader*, the weekly paper of the Independent Labour party, and she was a member of the influential 1917 Club, to which future prime min-

ister J. Ramsay MacDonald also belonged. Trudi had been blessed with a fine and powerful voice, and her contact with great orators like MacDonald, Lloyd George, and Bernard Shaw proved important in her development as a speaker.

This was an exciting and hopeful time for the young socialist to be in England. Trudi vividly remembers the night in December 1923 when Labour achieved the victory that would take it into power the next year. She waited with friends in Queens Hall and celebrated into the night as more and more results came in and the election was assured for MacDonald and the Labour party.

From England, Trudi traveled to Florence to study Italian and to continue her writing. On the first anniversary of the death of Giacomo Matteotti, the secretary of the Italian Socialist party murdered by Mussolini in 1924, the government arrested socialists all over Italy. Trudi was arrested with many others in Florence when her name was found on library checkout slips of certain "subversive books." She was interrogated for five hours, jailed for a week, and then deported to Switzerland.

At the border my future husband awaited me. We went immediately to Berne by train. This was where the trouble really began with my family. We were greeted by a big delegation of the socialist party with red banners and prominent speakers. From that moment, I knew my parents would never want me back at home, nor would I ever want to go there again.

She and Kurt were married a few days later.

For the next three years, Trudi worked with the Social Democratic party in Switzerland. She became the secretary of the women's section of the party and worked to reorganize that movement. Kurt was an active party member and later became a prominent socialist member of the Swiss parliament, and a judge in the supreme court. He and Trudi began to have personal and political differences, however, and when the chance came to tour Germany to deliver speeches for the Social Democratic party, Trudi accepted the opportunity, and her short marriage to Kurt Duby ended.

In her first years in Germany, it was acceptable for Trudi, as a foreigner, to be involved in politics. She traveled all over the country giving speeches and working to build up membership in the party. In a short time, however, she became dissatisfied with the conservative and unimaginative party leadership and annoyed by its increasing bureaucracy. When Trudi realized that the working class in Germany no longer supported the party, she joined other dissatisfied Social Democrats and dissidents from the Communist party to form the Socialist Workers party.

Working to build up the new party, Trudi took on an exhausting schedule, living on trains all week, and delivering speeches in different locations each evening. Often Nazi sympathizers would use the discussion period after a speech as an excuse for violent confrontation. To avoid leaving time for such discussion, Trudi would be forced to talk for hours, from the opening of the hall until the moment it legally closed. She began to drop her prepared texts and speak without notes. In Nazi strongholds like Essen the Socialist Workers party hired protection groups to defend against the brutal Nazi gangs. Trudi became a powerful speaker, but also began to dread the violence her speeches might incite.

It was a frightening experience for me to see how an audience, a mass of people, could be maneuvered with words. At times, I felt as if I had strings in my hands and could create a mass psychosis among the puppets out there simply by moving my fingers. Frankly this was a horrible feeling for me, and I had to be very careful. Many times after meetings, the audience would ask, "When do we fight, when do we go to the barricades?" I would have to calm them and explain the Nazis would tear us to pieces.

Immediately after Hitler was appointed chancellor of Germany in January 1933, Trudi entered into what she describes as a "marriage of convenience," a common practice at the time. Through this marriage, she became a German citizen and hoped to be able to continue her political organizing. When the Reichstag was burned in February of the same year, all opposition to the Nazi party had to go underground. By making copies of her articles and mailing them in many locations around Berlin, Trudi was able to send news of the brutality of the Nazi regime to the Swiss papers. She lived in Hitler's Germany four months on the black list, changing apartments every night, often just a step ahead of the soldiers on her trail.

Walking the streets of Berlin, I would see cars full of friends arrested by the Nazis and have to look away. You could talk to no one you knew in the streets. The Nazis would let someone free to follow them and arrest all of their friends. This was a terrible time. I had to get out!

Finally she was able to escape by using a passport loaned by a British friend who closely resembled her.

For the next five years, Trudi continued to work in politics. Because of her reputation as a speaker and antifascist organizer, she was called to Paris to join the international struggle against war and fascism centered there.

In 1939, as the war approached, Trudi made her first trip to the United States to begin to organize a women's world congress against war.

I was in the States only a few weeks, and when I returned to Paris, France had been sold to Hitler through Laval. In the beginning of the war I was in Paris. One day French agents arrested all the non-French antifascists they could find, and I was picked up too. After a week in jail, we were taken to a train station in Paris, and while we protested loudly, were loaded on a train for an unknown destination. I refused to move and had to be carried on that train. Very late that night, we arrived and were marched in the darkness for an hour up a steep slope. At one point I reached up and touched a sharp object—barbed wire—and I knew I was in a detention camp. Later we discovered we were in the south of France.

After five months, through a lobbying effort of the Swiss government, Trudi was freed by the French and allowed to return to Geneva. She was able again to obtain a Swiss passport by having her German marriage annulled, and she returned to the United States to raise funds for European refugees.

Mexico

By 1940, Trudi was prepared to leave the turmoil of European politics. Bitterly disappointed by what seemed the futility of the fight against fascism and the failure of the great powers to avoid the war that was sweeping Europe, she joined other social democrats, pacifists, communists, and Jewish refugees, and immigrated to Mexico, a country with a reputation for accepting refugees. Like other immigrants, she was obliged to pledge not to become involved in Mexican politics, but this was not a difficult oath for Trudi to make. She was ready to begin a new life and had no reason to take part in Mexican political affairs.

But in spite of her pledge, and perhaps in spite of herself, Trudi did become involved in Mexican politics. Rather than work directly for the political machine of a particular party as she had in Europe, she tried to effect change indirectly as a journalist, always looking for a cause, and finding one that occupied her completely in the Lacandon Maya and their jungle. Much like the enlightened protagonist in Carl May's novels she had read as a child, Trudi became the champion of a noble Indian people doomed by the demands of "civilization."

In 1940, Gertrude Duby was a striking woman with an equally striking personality. Photographs of her from that first year in Mexico show a small, handsome woman with dark hair and a fine complexion, elegantly dressed in her own stylish way. Friends from that time, some of whom had also known Trudi in Europe, describe her as beautiful both for her sharp features and her commanding presence—a self-confident and straightforward manner that seemed to draw people to her. She was a woman of strong opinions, and friends came to expect both her steadfast loyalty and volatile temper. Depending on whether or not one agreed with her, Trudi was considered either

1941 Trudi in Mexico City

obstinate or remarkably faithful to what she believed. She had a genuine interest in other people, treating both the government official and the poor worker with equal respect and judging both on equal terms.

Trudi was never a tourist in Mexico. From the first, she intended to become integrated into Mexican society, to make that country her home. Not long after her arrival in Mexico City, she impressed the secretary of labor, Ignacio García Tellez, who hired her as a social worker and journalist to study the working conditions for women in Mexico's most primitive factories. Trudi was paid little, but she was able to tour extensively the western states of Jalisco, Nayarit, and Sinaloa and began to develop an understanding of the country as a whole.

Later, while researching a series of articles on the women who had fought in Gen. Emiliano Zapata's revolutionary army, Trudi expanded her travels to other Mexican states: Morelos, where Zapata's struggle began, and

Puebla, Mexico, and Guerrero, where some of his soldiers were by then dispersed. She became deeply involved with the story of these women fighters, perhaps feeling a certain kindred spirit with their struggle to save their agrarian way of life.

More important for the purposes of this book, Trudi made her first photographs. For fifty pesos, she purchased an Agfa Standard Camera from another immigrant, a German-born actor named Blum. From Blum she also received her first rudimentary photographic training, the only technical instruction she ever had. He taught her the purpose of the aperture setting on her camera's one fixed lens and showed her the function of its few shutter settings. Blum cautioned her to avoid the harsh direct light of Mexico's midday sun and urged her to steer her subjects away from difficult backlit settings. In the darkroom, Blum taught her, in a rudimentary way, to make prints. From the outset, though, Trudi had no interest in the technical side of photography.

I am in every way a totally nontechnical person. If I look at a machine the wrong way, it will certainly break. To this day, I don't know what to say when people ask me what lens I use. I'm just not interested in that part of photography.

In her study of the *zapatistas*, as in her later photographs in the jungles of Chiapas, Trudi worked without benefit of a light meter, relying instead on the simple instructions on the film package as a guide in setting her shutter speed and aperture. Unlike the young Manuel Alvarez Bravo, whom she came to know in her first year in Mexico City, Trudi did not consider herself a serious photographer. Bravo became Mexico's best-known photographer and a subtle master of the photographic medium. In contrast, Trudi considered herself a journalist, and once she had learned enough to fix an image on film, she tried to ignore her uncomfortable but necessary alliance with this machine—her camera.

She approached the *zapatistas* in much the same bold and straightforward way she would later photograph the Lacandon Maya. There is, in fact, a staggering consistency of vision throughout her forty years with the camera. Trudi talked about this consistency one morning after some prodding from her editors, the only time we heard her analyze her photography.

It is very bad, probably, not to change as a photographer, but my character hasn't changed much either over the years. I think the character and the pictures go together.

On the boat to Mexico from America, Trudi had read the French anthropologist Jacques Soustelle's honest and loving account of his Mexican exploration in 1934, published in France under the title *Mexico, Tierre Indienne*. She took particular interest in a tribe called the Lacandones, whom Soustelle described as living a most primitive and remote existence in the dense jungles of southern Chiapas. Trudi decided that as soon as she could, she would find these people whom, unlike all other indigenous peoples of Mexico, the Spanish had not conquered and the Christian missionaries had not converted.

From Soustelle's book, Trudi learned that people called Lacandones had fought quite bitterly with the Spanish conquistadores and, after being scattered by several "punitive expeditions," had withdrawn to the interior of the huge rainforest that bordered Mexico and Guatemala. She learned, as well, that these few hundred farmers and hunters spoke a language similar to that of the three hundred thousand Mayans to the north in the Yucatán and still worshiped the ancient Mayan gods that predated the advent of Christianity. Soustelle described a Stone Age, polygamous culture, where men and women with uncut hair wore long white tunics, lived in simple huts, and hunted with bow and arrow.

In 1943, Trudi's dream of encountering the Lacandones was to be realized. The day she arrived in Chiapas with letters of recommendation for the governor, Dr. Rafael Gamboa, was also the beginning of her true assimilation into Mexican society. In his office in the capital city, Tuxtla Gutiérrez, Trudi asked Gamboa how she might visit the Lacandones. She learned that he had just sent out an expedition under the direction of Manuel Castellanos, the first governmental investigation of the century to the Lacandon jungle. The purpose of this expedition was to determine the living conditions of the Lacandones and to decide the need for governmental assistance. Gamboa felt the journalist and photographer might be a useful addition to the expedition and wired ahead to Castellanos to delay his departure until Trudi could join him in San Cristóbal, where final preparations were being made.

Several days later, in the northern Lacandon settlement of Puná (Monte Líbano), Trudi captured her first encounter with a Lacandon on film. On a hewn log at the edge of a big Lacandon tobacco field stood a tunic-clad man, as still as the leaves of the jungle that seemed to envelop him.

I looked up and suddenly realized a man, one human being, was standing there on a log. I had not seen or heard him come up. He seemed to be a part of that log, standing totally immobile and erect and melting into the forest. Finally he whistled into a leaf and other Lacandones appeared at the edge of the forest. These were all very small people and, unlike us, moved totally without noise. Suddenly they were behind me or near me without my having heard a sound. With their clothes and hair and silent footsteps, they seemed really part of the jungle.

Trudi had arrived in the jungle at a pivotal time for the Puná Lacandones and, for that matter, for other Lacandones of the northern and southern groups she would come to know. Except for a small amount of barter with the Tzeltal Indians and a few pesos received from the occasional sale of tobacco, these people lived much the same self-sufficient and isolated life of their ancestors. As Trudi and Castellanos were to witness on this first trip, these Lacandones still worshiped some of the ancient Mayan gods, burning copal incense to Hachäkyum, the god of the earth and sky, to Akinchop, the protector of the people from jungle beasts, and to K'ak', the forest god of fire.

The Lacandones had sporadic contact with loggers for much of the nineteenth and early twentieth centuries. By 1940, they had also come to feel the presence of the landless campesinos who arrived to establish permanent settlements on the edges of the Lacandon jungle. Yet the dense tropical forest remained an adequate barrier until 1960, when government logging companies for the first time used heavy equipment to cut roads through the middle of the jungle. The thousands of homesteaders who followed, themselves victims of Mexico's population explosion and inequitable land tenure, crowded the Lacandones deeper and deeper into the jungle. Many Lacandon leaders fell victim to disease, and the Christian missionaries who preached in the wake of those deaths promised salvation for all who abandoned the ancient Mayan gods.

On the 1943 expedition, without knowing it, Trudi was witnessing the beginning of the end of traditional Lacandon society, a gradual deterioration she came to record with her camera. This expedition, with the building of two sturdy houses given by the governor to the Lacandones, was the first scene in a drama to be acted out over the next four decades. During those years, Trudi made over twelve major expeditions to the Lacandon jungle of three to seven months each and over sixty shorter trips of five to twenty days. At one time, she knew almost every member of the two distinctly different groups of Lacandones: the northern group scattered over an enormous region between the Santa Cruz River and the Chocoljá River and the southern group of Cedro-Lacanjá.

On all her expeditions, Trudi did what she could to help the Lacandones, often saving one or another small group from disaster. She became an outspoken advocate of this people, fighting at first to try to keep intact the traditional Lacandon way of life and, when that seemed lost, waging an even more desperate and important battle to save their fragile jungle environment.

Trudi's advocacy of the Lacandones has earned her critics over the years, both within and outside Mexico's social science establish-

1943 Lacandon jungle, Trudi with southern Lacandones at chicle camp on the Cedro River

ment. Most accuse her of considering the needs of the few hundred Lacandones over those of the more numerous highland Maya of Chiapas. If she has on occasion been guilty of such partisanship, it is because she considers the Lacandones "family," and is treated by them with the same partiality. Watching Trudi greet Chan K'in Viejo of Najá, one sees clearly the special relationship. Trudi addresses Chan K'in as "father," and he responds by calling her "mother."

There are a few photographs from 1943 of Trudi with the Lacandones. Some of these snapshots could just as well have been made of old friends at a reunion, at ease with one another and already showing a great deal of mutual affection. Trudi was immediately drawn to these extremely proud and independent people. She found them to be scrupulously honest and generous, full of humor, and seemingly without greed or competitive impulses. Curiously, Trudi did not seem to experience the "culture shock" practically all fieldworkers describe on a first immersion into the daily life of another people. As a result one never senses a hesitant or tentative quality in her work, even in Trudi's first photographs from this expedition.

There is one thing that has helped me with all the Indians: I never saw them as different from me. They may have been different in their customs, but they were human beings, and I treated them as equals. I wasn't afraid of them either. Anthropologists are often afraid of offending them. Of course one should be careful not to offend and try to be tactful, but never be afraid. You know the story of fear anyway? If you are afraid of the gun, the gun goes off.

For twenty years, from 1943 to 1963, Trudi worked closely with her husband, cartographer and archaeologist Frans Blom. Frans had originally traveled to the jungles of southern Mexico in 1919 with an oil exploration firm and in 1925 first met the Lacandones during a Tulane University expedition near the important Mayan ruin at Palenque. With Oliver LaFarge, he published a two-volume account of this trip, *Tribes and Temples*, in 1926. By the time Trudi met Frans in 1943, he was a seasoned and well-known jungle explorer, responsible for the discovery of many significant Mayan ruins. He was also trying to build a new life in Mexico, fighting off recurring bouts with alcoholism that had ruined his academic career at Tulane, where he had directed the Middle American Research Institute during its early years.

By 1943, Trudi was also becoming well known in Chiapas and in Mexico City, where she sent many articles and photographs to be published. Her first book, a small pamphlet on the Lacandones, came out in that year. As the first white woman to travel in the jungle, she had begun to establish her reputation. When Frans met her on the airstrip at the town of Ocosingo, he readily made an exception to his rule of never allowing women on expeditions and invited her along.

1945 Frans Blom on expedition

Trudi's previous travels in the Lacandon jungle had not prepared her for what she faced on the 1943 expedition with Frans. The trip became a kind of test for Trudi, in which her courage and physical resources were stretched to the limit.

At first the expedition went well, as their small group searched for lost Mayan ruins and found opportunities to visit both the northern and southern Lacandones, who greeted the explorers warmly. Trouble began, however, when one of the pack mules fell and injured its leg. Trudi and Frans continued to look for more ruins while their helpers returned to the nearest town for another mule and supplies.

That night, as Trudi prepared dinner in camp, Frans began to show the first symptoms of malaria and refused to eat. On the trail the next morning, when Frans proved too ill to carry his supplies, Trudi devised a plan to go ahead with her own pack to the campsite, then double back, after several hours of difficult walking, to carry Frans's pack as well. In pitch darkness and hard

rain, she found Frans that night, tied into his hammock above the trail, and stayed with him until daybreak. Despite her relative inexperience, Trudi led him to the new camp, continued to care for him, and succeeded in rationing their meager supplies for the ten days before their helpers finally returned. Frans's diaries from that trip are filled with admiration and no small amount of affection for the courageous and levelheaded woman who, in all probability, had saved his life.

For most of the 1940s, Trudi and Frans were based in Mexico City and came to Chiapas whenever there was an assignment or funding could be raised for another expedition. In 1948 their most significant and difficult expedition of the decade took place—seven months on foot in the Lacandon jungle during a particularly wet rainy season. On this trip, Frans discovered two more important Mayan ruins, and Trudi, despite a bout with malaria, photographed extensively and added to her knowledge of both Lacandon groups. Out of this expedition came the material for the Bloms' two-volume study, *La Selva Lacandona* (The Lacandon jungle), published in 1955 and 1956 to detail their extensive archaeological and anthropological findings.

Finally in 1950, on the eve of their departure on yet another expedition, the Bloms purchased a house in San Cristóbal, which would be expanded over the next decade as a center for scientific studies for the state of Chiapas. Out of the Lacandones' confusion of the name Blom with their own word *balum*, meaning "jaguar," the house came to be called "The House of the Jaguar," or "Na Bolom" in the language of the highland Tzotzil.

The specific purpose of Na

Bolom, since its inception, has been to make Chiapas accessible to visiting students, scholars, and scientists. Later, the Bloms opened their home to any Lacandon who needed to come to San Cristóbal for medical help or supplies. A few rooms were also added for paying guests to help support the activities of the center. Trudi and Frans appreciated Chiapas art and textiles, and Frans was an expert on its archaeology. To keep significant artifacts within the state, they began to collect important examples from each of these fields. Today, Na Bolom contains a unique library of Mayan culture, a museum of Mayan archaeology and Lacandon culture, and a chapel housing an unequaled collection of religious art from the region. Since 1960, volunteers from all over the world have come for a year at a time to live and work at Na Bolom. For the last ten years, one of Trudi's closest friends, Ken Nelson, has coordinated all the activities of the center.

In 1975, with the proceeds of a large honorarium she received for an ecological lecture in Mexico City, Trudi established a nursery to grow native trees for free distribution to anyone willing to plant them within the state. As a result, twenty-five to thirty thousand trees are planted in the ravaged soil of the Chiapas highlands each year. Although Trudi sees this nursery as one of the solid accomplishments of her lifetime, she realizes this reforestation effort is miniscule in the face of the ongoing destruction of trees in both the highland forest and lowland jungle of Chiapas.

It is beyond the scope of this essay to list or detail all of Gertrude Blom's expeditions into this jungle or to begin to describe her close and long-lasting friendship with many individual Lacandones

1951 Agua Mula, Trudi and Frans in camp on the Viking Fund expedition

1952 El Real, Vicente Bor with K'ayum and K'in

ligious ceremonies Pancho K'in conducted to the Mayan gods. She also saw that this old man settled disputes, directed the planting of crops, and, above all, held the community together. Pancho K'in died the next year, and like other leaders of southern Lacandon communities, he took with him to the grave the greater part of the oral traditions of his people. Bor should have inherited his father's power, but he lacked the old leader's knowledge and prestige and had little authority with his people at Sakrum.

On expedition near the Jataté River in 1950, Trudi and Frans learned from a few crocodile hunters that Bor's people were starving a few miles downriver. With Pancho K'in's death, the correct cycle for burning fields and planting crops had been lost, and his descendants were barely holding on to life by eating the roots of jungle plants.

In the first of many instances in which she would save Bor from imminent disaster, Trudi gave his group all her expedition supplies and immediately organized an airlift of food and medicines to assist them through another year. She was deeply disturbed, however, to find that even with these new supplies, Bor and the other Sakrum Lacandones quarreled and appeared to be bitter rivals. She noted as well that they neglected to construct any god houses, so central to the life of all Lacandon communities at the time.

In 1952, on the edge of the jungle at the end of another expedition, Trudi found Bor with his two young sons, K'in and K'ayum, all terribly sick and helpless. The rest of Bor's large family had perished. One of his wives had fled to the Tojolobal region of Chiapas with

who have lived there. Perhaps, though, her forty-year relationship with the Lacandones can be illustrated by the story of one Lacandon man, Bor Wech Yuk, whose life and fate were so closely enmeshed with hers.

Trudi met Bor in 1946, at Sakrum, a small settlement deep in the southern Lacandon jungle. She was introduced to both of Bor's wives and his five children, and within a few hours was sitting down to a meal with them in Bor's simple hut perched dramatically between two white, jagged rocks above the Jataté River.

From her first descriptions of Bor, it is not difficult to see why Trudi was so quickly taken with him. Bor was an extremely proud and outgoing young man, warmhearted and full of humor. He had a sparkle in his eye, and an engaging and exuberant manner. With his self-assured manner and his classic Mayan features, Bor resembled some of the Lacandones Trudi had admired in Soustelle's *Mexico, Tierre Indienne*.

At that time, Bor's father, Pancho K'in, was the unquestioned patriarch of the thirty-four Lacandones at Sakrum. Trudi was allowed to witness some of the re-

her children, and all later died there of disease. Bor's other wife and infant had died during the grueling search for the missing family members. Trudi took Bor, K'in, and K'ayum back to San Cristóbal and nursed them back to health. But this first trip to town was to change the lives of all three.

For the next eight years, Bor lived in a kind of limbo, no longer able to exist in harmony with his small group in the jungle but incapable of adjusting to life in town. Each time his problems in the jungle became overbearing, Bor returned to Na Bolom, and Trudi always managed to help. For a time, Bor was married to his young niece Margarita, but she became so attracted to life in San Cristóbal, and so resentful of Bor for forcing her to go back with him to the jungle, that she left him for his brother.

Finally, in 1961, Trudi organized an expedition to establish Bor with a group of southern Lacandones at Lacanjá and purchased gifts and provisions for the trip. The Lacanjá people accepted Bor immediately and within a short time gave him two beautiful young wives. Like all the other southern Lacandones who had lost their leaders, Bor soon converted to Christianity. When he died in 1978, it is probable that Bor was the first in a thousand-year lineage of Lacandon patriarchs to have abandoned the traditional Mayan gods.

Unlike their father, K'in and K'ayum had remained in San Cristóbal and were immensely attracted to the life there. With Bor's permission, Trudi had enrolled the boys in separate schools in town. During much of their adolescence they lived at Na Bolom, for all practical purposes, as Trudi's adopted sons. As adults, however, neither was able to fully assimilate into the life of San Cristóbal, nor was either ever comfortable with his own people in the jungle.

The story of Bor's family is not an isolated one. All the Lacandones have experienced the anguish of a difficult and confusing forty-year transition from the Stone Age to the twentieth century; with the exception of a few stalwart northern Lacandones, all have abandoned their traditional values and religion. The deterioration of the Lacandon culture and the devastation of their jungle have been disappointing and frustrating for all who have witnessed these transformations, but especially so for Gertrude Blom, who has fought so long and hard to preserve the region from destructive change. Only in the remarkable photographic record she has compiled does the old way of life survive, and that is why, ultimately, Blom's photographs have seemed such a failure to her.

At eighty-two, Gertrude Blom is not one to live in the past. But in one of the last interviews Margaret and I conducted with her, Blom looked back over her life with no small amount of disappointment in her voice.

I was a fighter all my life, but that's a sad story. I tried to change the world without much success. The Nazis came; then we tried to avoid the war and the war came. I fought for the Lacandones and the forest and that's lost too."

Though Blom would choose to leave behind a better world, there is certainly some victory in the powerful and lasting record that is part of her legacy. In the final analysis, she should be judged not by the number of her victories or defeats but by the magnitude of her battles and the courage and integrity with which she has fought. For those who will continue to struggle with the problems of this deeply troubled century, perhaps Gertrude Blom's example as a fighter will prove her most important legacy.

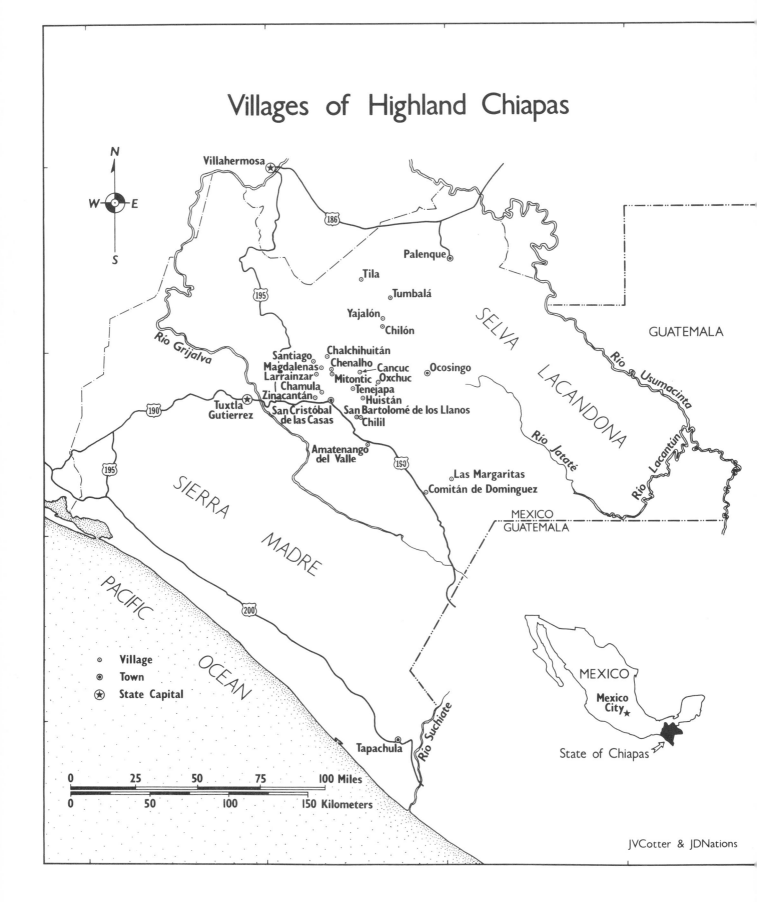

Villages of Highland Chiapas

Villahermosa

Palenque
Tila
Tumbalá
Yajalón
Chilón
Chalchihuitán
Santiago
Magdalenas
Chenalho
Cancuc
Ocosingo
Larrainzar
Mitontic
Oxchuc
Chamula
Tenejapa
Zinacantán
Huistán
Tuxtla
Gutierrez
San Cristóbal
de las Casas
San Bartolomé de los Llanos
Chilil
Amatenango
del Valle
Las Margaritas
Comitán de Dominguez

Río Grijalva

SELVA LACANDONA

Río Usumacinta

GUATEMALA

Río Jataté

Río Lacantún

MEXICO
GUATEMALA

SIERRA MADRE

PACIFIC OCEAN

○ Village
◉ Town
✪ State Capital

MEXICO

Mexico
City ★

State of Chiapas

Tapachula
Río Suchiate

0	25	50	75	100 Miles
0	50	100		150 Kilometers

JVCotter & JDNations

Tzotzil and Tzeltal: Who in the World?

Robert M. Laughlin

We were dropped off at the modern clinic in Chilil, a hamlet set at the edge of a pine forest. Its one-room houses had high-peaked roofs whose pine shingles were now mossy with age. We had been told that all the native doctors here had been accused of witchcraft and killed. Strong, hostile stares greeted us. No one spoke as we dumped our belongings on the clinic cots. "Where can we buy tortillas?" we asked. "No one sells tortillas here," we were told. And then the rain began. It poured through the joints in the tin roof. Soon we were standing in inches of water. This was as foreign to my companion from Mexico City as to me. It was several days before people would speak to us, and when they did, it was to exclaim, "Are you *still* here?" In the morning they were too busy to be disturbed by an anthropologist's nosy questions, and in the afternoon it rained, always. At last one family agreed to feed us tortillas and beans for a small fee, but they never ate with us. One day as we sat eating our humble fare before the wood fire, the mist sifting in between the wall planks, a visitor called out. Our host, sitting with his back to the door, shouted his lengthy reply without ever bothering to turn around. Neither of us could catch more than a word or two of their staccato language that sounded so different from Spanish. We endured a few more days of loneliness, wet, and cold and then retreated to the comforts of San Cristóbal. Yet we are both still anthropologists, and neither can throw off his fascination with the Indians living in the mountains of central Chiapas.

Undaunted by the unfriendliness of Chilil, I decided one day to try out Zinacantán. I had come to know two men from that town who worked in the National Indian Institute center in San Cristóbal. I thought I would ask one for lodging for the night. Setting out on foot for the two-hour walk, I took a wrong turn and landed in Chamula. A short time before, a German artist who could not communicate either in Spanish or the native language, Tzotzil, had strayed there. After chasing after some women to ask his way, he had been dispatched by men with machetes. That story was on my mind as I asked directions in halting Tzotzil from a *man*. When I reached the courthouse in Zinacantán, by chance I found one of my friends, who directed me to the other's thatch-roofed house, perched high on a slope. I had to find my way through a maze of muddy tracks that cut through the towering corn plants that formed a bewildering bright green jungle. When I called out timidly in the dusk, my friend leapt through the door. His suggestion that I sleep in the clinic rejected, he was forced to invite me in, perhaps the first time that an American had slept in an Indian house in Zinacantán. Accustomed to the Ladinos' (non-Indians) scorn for Indian ways, he offered me a meal with many apologies. As I sat eating, his wife and mother fired questions at him, while his daughter pressed close to her mother and stared wild-eyed at me. Over and over I heard the word *Lakantone*, at which my host roared with laughter. He had told them that a strange creature, a Lacandon Indian, was working in San Cristóbal, and they thought it must be me. "Oh no, Lacandons have *long* hair," he said, and he explained

1974 Santiago, Tzotzil men in front of the church

how we gringos were not like the local Ladinos, but treated the Indians as "brothers."

My host, Chep, offered me a drink of cane liquor as we sat by the fire, in the dim light of a kerosene lamp. Each time the baby cried, it was offered the breast through a slit in the side of its mother's blouse. Periodically the little girl, Maruch, was led off to bed by her grandmother, but within minutes she would be back at the fire, silently studying my face. The parents were very indulgent. Maruch was kept happy with peanut brittle brought from San Cristóbal. Even when her baby brother, Maryan, broke a pottery bowl, the parents only laughed.

There were two other members of the family—a black kitten and a lean, white dog. The kitten sat on the floor between my host's widely planted feet. Every so often he would absentmindedly flick the kitten's ears, one up, one down. The bitch's presence, though, was barely tolerated. It was the target of any small sticks or corncobs that lay close to Maruch or her grandmother.

We went to bed at eight, the hut wrapped in a blanket of cricket song, in the distance flute and drum and barking dogs. At 4:30

A.M., Chep's wife, Mal, sat up on her plank bed, adjusted her blouse, stood up, unloosed her sash, rearranged the folds of her full skirt, retied the sash, and stepped down to the floor. She bent over, hoisted Maryan up on her back, took her peppermint-striped shawl, held one end in her teeth and reached around to adjust the other end so Maryan was safely packaged, then tied the ends above her chest. The two went outside, then returned. Mal lit the fire and shifted Maryan to her lap, removing his woolen skirt and inner cloth. She held a clean cloth up to the fire to warm, played fondly with his genitals, wrapped him snugly, and hoisted him back up on his perch. After Mal fetched a pail of water to soak the corn and cook the beans, the silence of the dimly lit room was broken by the repeated swish, swish of the corn as she tossed handful after handful into the water and briefly swirled it around. Mal tossed the beans into another pot. Rinsing off the grinding stone and the wooden platform beneath it, she began grinding the corn. A half hour later the old woman joined her daughter-in-law, kneeling opposite her, regrinding her corn. The two women faced each other, their coppery features lit by the yellow lamp flame, their backs rhythmically waving back and forth, grinding, grinding, while two black eyes peeped out of a shawl. Hardly a word had been uttered.

When the corn was ground, the women formed it into lumps of dough, which they flattened into saucer-sized circles with heavy rims. Then they patted out the rims between their hands until the tortillas were dinner-plate size, ready to be placed on the round clay griddle to toast.

When Chep and I arose after six, a stack of steaming tortillas awaited us. We pulled our tiny chairs close to the fire, and after rinsing our mouths and washing our hands we were served bowls of cold beans, hard-boiled eggs, salt, tortillas, and sweetened coffee. No cutlery here! A piece of tortilla rolled into a scoop served as a spoon. This was not difficult with the egg, but spooning out the beans from their juice before the spoon disintegrated required great skill. The unsuspecting visitor is stuffed with soggy scraps of tortilla long before his bowl of beans is finished. After the meal we again washed our mouths and rinsed our hands.

A visitor thanks his host and is expected then to announce his departure several times. Each announcement is met with a polite "Are you going?" Following proper protocol, I bowed then to the grandmother who touched my head lightly with the back of her right hand. I slipped my hand briefly into my host's and departed.

Returning a year later to Zinacantán, I stayed in another household, determined to learn Tzotzil and become familiar with the culture. In graduate school we were told that when we were "in the field," we should go visiting from house to house. When I suggested that I pay a visit to our neighbors, I was asked, "Why?" My explanation was met with a howl of laughter while they debated how large a bottle of cane liquor I should take with me. Finally, with great condescension they offered me the explanation: "Here we don't go to see the face, here we go for a purpose, and we present a large bottle if it is a matter of importance, a small bottle if not." Desperate to escape from the smoke-filled house, I suggested then that I take a walk in the woods. This, too, was met with incredulity. "Walk in the woods? That's where the murderers roam!"

The outsider who wishes to peer into the culture and live it as best he can must do so with drink in hand. He must drink to see, and yet must have a "big head" so that his vision will not be blurred, nor his senses lost. I recall returning with a new-won friend from my first wedding at dusk, so fueled with cane liquor that I groped my way through a weaving, green, submarine landscape, until I stepped through the door and toppled to the floor. The next morning I learned to my satisfaction that my Indian companion had spent the night in the ditch. Gradually I found that that was an exception, as I watched Indians consume bottle after bottle with no visible effect, or watched them dance for hours and then walk the next morning down the mountain to their corn fields.

Only the man who drinks alone is an alcoholic, and every bottle must be shared equally by all present—there is no secret discarding of liquor. Food, too, must be shared equally. Once when we brought a roll of lifesavers, they were broken in half so all the children could have their share.

In Zinacantán there is a proper way to say and to do everything. Every word, every act, is scrutinized to the last detail. Our way of talking and acting was not different—it was wrong! So when my teacher, Romin, accompanied me to the house of a weaver to request that she weave me a black robe, my heart was in my throat, knowing I must carry out the transaction without fault. We approached the thatch-roofed house and suddenly slowed our steps

(properly) as we reached her yard. Romin turned to me with a wink and an owlish smile as he exclaimed in English, "Goood luck!"

These people who stare so directly at the camera, who march in processions totally absorbed in their devotion to the saints on parade, what do we know of their past?

One looks in vain for majestic pyramids. Around 500 A.D. there came an influx of people to the highlands of Chiapas. At this time the Mayan language of the intruders split into two languages, Tzotzil and Tzeltal (whose difference might be compared to that between Spanish and Portuguese). Both groups constructed cliff-top forts with houses set on a series of high terraces. Occasionally they boasted a ball court, but there is little evidence of luxury. These mountain fastnesses persisted until the arrival of the Spaniards. The only written record of life in Chiapas before the Spanish assault tells how Aztec merchant spies, donning Zinacantec clothing and speaking Tzotzil, traded obsidian blades and needles for amber and quetzal feathers, always fearful that their true identity would be discovered and they would be quickly killed.

The first Spanish expedition reached the highlands in 1524 after a fierce battle with the lowland Chiapanecs, whose rivals were the Zinacantecs, lords of the highlands and controllers of a salt monopoly. The highlanders accepted the Spaniards with no resistance until a Spanish soldier traveled on his own to Chamula and demanded gold. Unsatisfied with his gifts, he seized the chief, and the Chamulas rose up in rebellion. Captain Marín sent that soldier walking 108 leagues to

Mexico City to be punished by Cortés, but Chamula was not appeased. Tossing golden diadems from the parapets, they shouted down to the Spanish invaders, "You like gold? Come in, because we have lots here!" as they heaved caldrons of boiling water and blood, clubs, and lances at the men below. Had it not been for the aid of the Zinacantecs, the Spaniards would have been decimated, but at last, in a downpour and thick fog, the Chamulas abandoned their fortress. Peace was made, and the Spanish retired to the coast. Not until 1528, in an expedition under the command of Diego de Mazariegos, did the Spanish bring the highlands under their control.

In 1545 a band of Dominican friars settled in Zinacantán, burned the idols, and built a church. Though complaining of spending nights in Indians' huts, sharing their beds with crying babies, scurrying mice, squawking hens, and crawling lice, they sought to convert the Indians to Christianity, and they soon became their ardent defenders. Their struggles to lessen the Indians' hardships were vigorously supported by the first bishop of Chiapas, Bartolomé de Las Casas, who entrusted his gold watch and library to Zinacantán as he departed for Spain to carry his mission to King Charles V.

From entries in a colonial Tzotzil dictionary emerges a vision of the medieval European world carried to Chiapas: wineskins and greyhounds, jesters and jousts, curry combs and falcon's fetters. But they also tell the darker side: dungeons and racks, pillories and gallows, tribute and servitude. The hardships of the colonial period sparked miraculous events: a Virgin's descent from Heaven and her promise to aid the Indians, who responded by building a chapel in her honor and offering her food and incense. Three times this was repeated in the early eighteenth century. The final appearance in Cancuc in 1712, in a time when the local bishop was burdening the populace with exorbitant demands for tribute, provoked a revolt by thirty-two towns. Spanish priests were ousted and replaced by Indians, Cancuc was renamed New Spain, and the king declared dead. Three Indians became kings of Cancuc. But within a year, the Spanish army, undeterred by the magic employed against it, quelled the rebellion. By the eighteenth century the Dominican friars had established a huge network of cattle and sugarcane ranches on whose edges lived the miserable Indian labor force.

Independence from Spain provided no relief to the Indians. Control fell into the hands of "the Chiapas Family," one hundred Ladino families who perpetuated the division between Indian and Ladino societies. First they made "legal" claim to all Indian forest land, and indeed to any land not strictly in the center of Indian communities. Families already settled on those lands suddenly discovered that they were required now to provide a month of labor to their new landlords. Then they carved up the Church lands, including the land of the Indian religious brotherhoods.

In 1867 a Virgin appeared in Chamula. As in Cancuc, divine intervention inspired new efforts to make Christianity truly Indian and incited the Indians to open warfare against their oppressors. The Chamulas and their converts from nine other towns marched on San Cristóbal and penetrated the out-

skirts. Then, even though they far outnumbered the defenders, they mysteriously withdrew. Their cult faded away, leaving behind, nevertheless, a native priesthood and a degree of religious freedom. San Cristóbal was left in a state of panic. A century later, the whispered, though false, alarm "The Chamulas are coming!" caused Ladinos to shutter their windows.

The historical accounts portray the Chamulas as so barbaric in 1867 that they urged the people not to worship white gods, but instead to crucify an Indian boy of their own and worship him. In fact, this myth (still believed by many today) was created twenty years later when plans were afoot to move the capital from San Cristóbal. The intellectuals took up their pens to portray their city as the bulwark of civilization against the barbarians.

In 1911, in the early days of the revolutionary period, staunchly conservative San Cristóbal, despite its fear of Chamulas, did not hesitate to support the bishop when he provided the Indians with arms to attack the liberal lowland Ladinos. Led by "Pajarito" (little bird), they aroused great terror in the populace, both Indian and Ladino. After one of the last battles the liberal army captured eight Chamulas and, employing a punishment "in harmony with their rudimentary understanding," cut off their ears as a lesson to their compatriots that "civilization" would prevail (L. Espinosa, 1912: 152). Apparently, they borrowed the idea from the Italians, who, according to newspaper reports that had reached Chiapas, had practiced it on the Turks in the Italo-Turkish War.

In Chiapas, however, the battles of the Revolution were waged pri-

marily in Zinacantán with little loss of life, though memories of the first airplanes and of the musical instruments abandoned on the field are still strong. The revolutionary government's violent attacks on the Church forced the Indians to hide their saints in the forest for protection against the "god burners." There they worshiped in secret until they could return their saints to their "homes."

For all the touting of the Revolution as the force that returned the land to the people, this process did not begin in Chiapas until many years later (the 1930s). Because of their landless state the Indians were easy marks for the Ladino coffee plantation owners. From the late nineteenth century to the 1940s Ladinos employed by the plantations lured Indians from the highlands to work in the tropics. With the connivance of the Ladino mayors or town clerks of the Indian communities, they set up their tables in the town plazas, where they sat before heaps of silver pesos and contracted their workers. After receiving a first payment, the newly recruited workers were shaved and transported in trucks and on foot to the Pacific coast plantations, where they were housed three tiers high in fetid dormitories. Overworked, underfed, malaria ridden, their meager pay exhausted in the company store, many resolved to escape and return home on foot. The terrible journeys on mountain trails were almost inevitably interrupted by bands of Ladino highwaymen, who would strip the poor unfortunates of their last centavos. Memories from his childhood of these Indians collapsing along the roadside impelled one Ladino, Manuel Castellanos, to become

1946 Manuel Castellanos assisting voter registration of Chamula Indians (*Tzotzil*)

the major defender of the Indians in the 1930s, 1940s, and 1950s.

It was mainly Tzotzils who labored in the coffee plantations, while their neighbors, the Tzeltals, were slaving to the east, in the Lacandon jungle, chopping the giant trees to provide Americans and Europeans with fine mahogany beds, tables, and bureaus. The suffering of the Tzeltals is graphically described in the novels of B. Traven.

In 1951, when the National Indian Institute arrived in San Cristóbal to set up education, medical, and agricultural programs for the Indians, the directors of the institute were accused of being communists. At that time Indians were not allowed on the sidewalks and were jailed if found in town after sunset. Ten years later Ladinas still stationed themselves at the entrances to San Cristóbal at dawn to waylay the incoming Indians, grabbing their chickens and vegetables and giving them a few centavos in return. To see Indians kicked into the backs of second-class buses was not unusual.

No longer today do Indians travel to San Cristóbal with fear in their hearts; no longer do they ex-

pect that any surprise encounter with a Ladino will lead to their death. They are more worldly wise, more willing to seek work in distant places, eager to strike up conversations with Ladinos and to stare into the eyes of Ladina girls. Now they dare to challenge the authorities of church and state. But though all would agree that their fathers and grandfathers suffered greater hardships, they are not at peace with the present.

"Everything is changing, nothing is the same now," they say. "The schools knock down our culture. The young people have learned to speak Spanish. They read and write, but they are forgetting our customs. Some men are rich, they own trucks, they travel to Mexico City, but they refuse to serve our gods. Punishment will come. We will all die in the year 2000."

It is a time of turmoil in the highlands of Chiapas. Frans Blom often remarked, "I want to die before all the Indians wear polyester and all the *gringos* wear Indian clothes." Not all yet, but many, fulfill that dark vision. While the loss of traditional clothing is the most apparent change, other changes cause more cultural havoc. The cash economy has invaded the society, so that houses formerly loaned are now rented, prospective brides who once were presented for two years with gifts of food and drink before the wedding may now be bought on the spot, native doctors whose services were remunerated with tortillas, chickens, and cane liquor may now demand payment in thousands of pesos cash.

Where once everyone belonged to the Partido Revolucionario Institucional and solved their disputes within the framework of the establishment political party, now

many reach out in frustration to any party that will help them, whether reactionary, socialist, or communist. In the past all local disputes and crimes (except murder) were handled by the magistrate of each community, but now the culprits and the plaintiffs run for support to a host of competing lawyers and government agencies.

The Catholic religion, molded by the Mayan ancestors into a new Mayan Christianity, has also been under attack. Energetic European priests have preached reform, urging the people to abandon their saints and concentrate on Christ and the Virgin Mary, to abandon also the traditional holy days with their skyrockets, banquets, and bottles of cane liquor. Evangelical Protestant missionaries from the United States, too, have converted many from their traditional beliefs and practices. Refusing to cooperate in the town fiestas, abstaining from hard liquor, convinced they have a chance at immortality on earth, these converts have been driven out of their communities and forced to squat around the commercial center of San Cristóbal.

Economic crisis is not a novelty in Chiapas, but population pressures have pushed many Indians from their mountain houses to cut and burn a place in the distant jungle. Those who rented land for corn farming at the foot of their mountains now must travel by bus or truck for many hours to reach available land. The search for wage labor, too, has carried young men into the oil fields of Tabasco and even to the nuclear plant in northern Veracruz.

While the Tzeltal and Tzotzil towns of Chiapas share many customs and attitudes, there is tre-

1963 San Miguel Mitontic Festival, Chamula woman and child (*Tzotzil*)

mendous diversity. Each town has its own costume of daily dress. Some towns are monogamous; in others men may have several wives. In some towns women are rarely seen drunk in public; in others it is a frequent occurrence. The ritual bowing of Zinacantecs is laughed at by the Chamulas. Tenejapan girls compose and sing bold sexual songs to challenge the young men. Unthinkable in Zinacantán!

These cultural differences are the despair of the government bureaucrat assigned to carry out a project in the highlands. A public works project in Oxchuc will be met with the greatest cooperation of the townspeople, while the same project in Chamula may be met by unyielding opposition. And in Zinacantán they will argue endlessly until they have acquired the most for the least.

Perhaps most frustrating for the government agent is the language barrier, for although the Indians are learning Spanish, it is a very rare bureaucrat or technician who attempts to learn the Indian languages. Only the priests have approached a mastery of Tzeltal or Tzotzil.

Throughout Mexico, while Spanish and English are called "languages," Indian languages are termed mere "dialects," and yet Tzotzil (with several dialects and subdialects of its own) boasts a vocabulary of over thirty thousand words. While it borrowed many words from Spanish to name the objects introduced by the colonists and by the modern industrial world, Tzotzil is rich in terms to describe sounds and shapes. There are words to describe the sound of a pig chomping peach pits, of a mature woman peeing and a virgin peeing, of a truck grinding up a steep slope. The same term describes a woman's messy hair and the thatch of a roof blown awry in a wind storm. Another may refer to the swelling of weevil-eaten beans when boiled and to the swelling of one's bee-stung body.

Witness the lyrical quality of Tzotzil terms for emotion:

I relent
I hold my heart aloft

I please you
I perfume your heart

I am enraged
My heart is swarming

I am fickle
I am of many hearts.

The prayers spoken at home, at church, or in the mountain shrines, prayers that are spoken in couplets at high speed, create a code. Things are not what they seem.

The fiery heart,
   The crimson heart   a witch
Your lordly sunbeams,
   Your lordly shadows   corn
Our flower,
   Our leaf   cane liquor
A sliver of Your passion,
   A splinter of Your cross   money.

When religious officials meet to celebrate a fiesta, they are required to entertain their fellows and their gods with a back-and-forth banter of off-color lines and double entendres, striving to outdo their companions. Laughter is a basic ingredient of Mayan Christianity.

This Christianity, for so long a major strength of the Indian people of Chiapas, is not a veneer concealing a pagan world. Rather it is a synthesis of Christian and Mayan beliefs. Christ is the creator of all things, but after his crucifixion he rose to heaven as the sun and he brought the flood as punishment. For replying rudely to Christ when he asked them how they had weathered the flood, all but one of the survivors were turned into monkeys and jaguars. From that one survivor's rib a woman was made, and after the devil taught them the ways of the world, a child was born. Christ and his mother, the moon, travel through the sky watching mankind. They and the saints, who emerged miraculously from deep caves, together with the spirits of the first ancestors, who reside in the mountains, care for the people. But the task is not easy, as the Earth Lords, who also dwell in the mountains, are eager to buy human souls from witches and condemn them to work on their plantations. Unless the people have lived a good life, they cannot win the protection of the gods. Unless the saints' days and other religious holidays are celebrated, the townspeople will be punished by drought, famine, and poverty. So in every town the saints are brought out on procession by the religious officials dressed in their finery according to the positions they hold. For one year the official serves, offering prayers, jokes, candles, flowers, skyrockets, incense,

1956 Chenalhó, Saint's procession (Tzotzil)

1967 Tenejapa, Prayer and curing ceremonies in the church (Tzeltal)

liquor, banquets, song, and dance. Deeply in debt at the end of his term, he may decide not to serve again; or when he has recovered his fortune, he might serve a second, third, or fourth time, rising in prestige with each step.

Also guardians of the community are the shamans, the local doctors who by their dream power realized that they could serve as lawyers for the defense of their clients, pleading their cases before the gods. By reading his patient's pulse, the shaman diagnoses the illness and determines what prayers are appropriate and which herbs should be prepared. He offers prayers, geraniums, candles and incense, Coca Cola and cane liquor. Black chickens are sacrificed for man and gods.

In some towns curing ceremonies are performed at home and at church. In others, as in Zinacantán, the curing party may also visit a circuit of mountain shrines, often in the dead of night. Their way lit by flashlights or a Coleman lantern, the party winds its way single file up the frost-whitened trail. Men and women wrapped in black woolen robes or shawls exhale clouds of steam. The assistants march at the head of the trail, one carrying a basket of flowers on

his back, another carrying a censer and a handful of incense, a third carrying a net filled with clanking liquor bottles, and the last assistant carrying the candles. The patient comes next, followed, at the very end, by the shaman bearing his bamboo staff.

Arriving at the crosses, the assistants tie bunches of geraniums to the pine boughs that have already been fastened to the crosses. Shaman and patient kneel while the shaman lines up the candles. In the flickering light streams of couplets roll on and on, begging forgiveness and pleading protection from the gods. Should a moth be attracted to the flames, it is quickly batted down, for who knows if it is not a spy sent by the witch who cast the sickness. A round of drinks is served at the beginning, middle, and end of the prayers. A swallow of the fiery, clear liquor banishes for a moment the night chill as the party kneels briefly before the tall crosses and sets off for the next shrine.

Among the Tzotzil and Tzeltal natural illness is possible only for the very old. True, some can drink themselves to death, but usually another individual is considered responsible for the sickness, is the agent of sickness. For this reason it is extremely important to pay close attention to one's dreams, for it is in the dream world that man can communicate with the gods and must struggle against his enemies. Here his enemies are revealed to him. Here, too, he is given signs to foresee his future: enter a red car—become sick with chills and fever; see corn in heaps—have a good harvest; be attacked by a cow—be tormented by a witch. Many, many images have standard interpretations known throughout the community. Here

the daily anxieties are enacted with dramatic force:

God, My Lord, I, Romin Teratol, dreamt just before dawn, on Sunday, the twenty-third of June.

Well, it seemed that I was at Ak'ol Ravol. I was with some Chamulas there—there at the church. "Go, Romin," a Chamula said to me, "Go, bring this!" he said, but it wasn't clear what I was to bring—just, "Go, go and bring it, because it is needed very badly right now," he told me. And he gave me a black cow. I mounted it. I went to bring whatever it was that was needed. Quickly I mounted it. I went off to bring it. I was there at the white house, just there inside the meadow, but the black cow was flying terribly high, it seemed. It jumped over the fences, the tall trees, everything.

Then on the return trip, the cow gored me. My leg was pierced, but lots of blood flowed from my leg. But the cow spoke to me. "I will cure your leg," she said.

"But will it get well?" I asked.

"It will get well. It won't take long to cure," she said. And she began to lick my leg. It got well immediately.

And then I woke up. But when I awoke, I tried to figure out what my dream meant.

Then I started to tell my wife what my dream meant.

And, "Who knows what it means?" she told me. Just in joking she told me, "Probably it's because you are a witch. *Why would you dream of black cows?*" she said to me.

But I think probably it's a bit of torment. That's what I tell myself, "*Because I was given a black cow to mount,*" I say to myself.

And that's the way it all is (Laughlin, 1976: 34).

It is a very small leap from the dream world to the folktales, some of which are considered to be true history and some to be for entertainment or the presentation of moral lessons. These tales, like the religion, are a synthesis of Spanish and Mayan elements reworked according to the genius of the people. Brer Rabbit and Cinderella vie with the saints, spooks, demons, buzzard men, magic bells and magic wands, kings and highwaymen, Earth Lords and Earth Lords' serpentine daughters.

Once there was a poor boy, but he was really a king. He used to go and play on the side of Muxul Vitz. He would fiddle around with the sand. He went every day. One day he found a ring buried there.

He went home. Then he went to borrow a pot. The next morning all the pots, water jugs, and hearth pots, all of them were filled with money. The king was now a very rich man.

The Mexicans heard about it. They came to lead him away with music, with marimbas, rockets, and a fiesta. He left very grandly.

The people of the town here assembled. The people of our town scattered a lot of money.

The San Cristóbal people strew pine needles. That's why they stayed richer. The king was allowed to choose a wife. "Hide the ring here," he told his wife. She swallowed it.

They left. The woman, too. They slept by the road. A mouse arrived. Quickly it stuck its tail up the girl's nose. The girl sneezed right away. She farted. The ring

came out. The mouse took it away. A cat went and took it from him. Then they chased wildly after the mouse until the king, himself, got the ring.

Then the king put it on his finger. He didn't give it to anyone else anymore. He arrived in Mexico City (and never came back). That's why the Mexicans are richer (Laughlin, 1977: 77).

This same magic and surrealism, so pervasive in dream and myth, also animate the fiestas. Men dress up as monkeys, race in horse races with no winners, run on fire, stand stock still to strike a jousting target, kill a straw bull and drink its blood of cane liquor seasoned with onion, mint, and chili, or engage in a battle of horse manure. Reenacted every year, these dramatic events in many instances recall historical scenes, in a history that is circular, repetitive. Yesterday is today and will be tomorrow.

It was not without fear twenty years ago that Romin Teratol and Anselmo Peres agreed to travel with me to the United States, for everyone in Zinacantán knew that the people who lived at the edge of the earth ate their babies.

The first welcome across the border was not encouraging.

ROMIN:
As for me, I had brought fifty pesos of my money to buy things to eat. I asked them to change it for me there. But me, I hadn't realized that our money would lose value there. When I saw the change for my money, there were only four pesos, four dollars, as they say.

When I took the change for my money, "Where's the rest?" I asked.

"What do you mean, are you going to change more?" they asked me.

"No more, just the fifty," I said.

"But that's complete, like that," they told me. The fifty pesos of my money came out to four pesos now, but I had

thought I would use it to supplement the food for my stomach, if my stomach wasn't kept full, but how could you do it since it turned into four pesos? But it was used up on soft drinks on the way. It never reached the place where I was going, because the money shrivelled up on the way (Laughlin, 1980: 35–36).

ANSELMO:
It just vanished. *We were confused because we didn't know about the money there. We just asked you how much each coin was worth.*

"There are fifty-cent pieces, there are quarters, there are dimes, there are nickels, there are pennies," you told us. You showed us what the money was like.

"Ah!" we said, since we are dumb Indians. We didn't know about the money of the white gents (Laughlin, 1980: 96–97).

Then came the first meal at a restaurant.

ROMIN:
The woman handed us the menu to find out what kind of food we wanted. But it was all in English. But as for us, we didn't understand it. We simply stood up. "Never mind, we won't eat," we said to ourselves, because it was already time for work, too. We had already stood up.

But the thing was, there was a man standing there who knew Spanish. "What do you want?" he said.

"We want our meal, but we don't understand English," we said.

"No, I'll ask for it myself. What do you want to eat?" said the man.

"Well, we want beans and meat," we said.

The kind old man quickly asked for our meal, but by word of mouth not by looking at the paper. If it hadn't been for the man standing there we wouldn't have eaten before work. It was just that the man standing there did us the favor. The next day we didn't go looking for meals anymore in other places, only where they knew Spanish. We didn't change around at all anymore.

The place where we went to work, the office, was awfully hot, because the building was heated. We simply sweated and sweated (Laughlin, 1980: 36–37).

On Thanksgiving Day we went to the Episcopal Church.

ROMIN:

Well, on Thursday, the twenty-eighth of November, we went to Mass where those who don't worship God properly, hold Mass. But they didn't celebrate a proper Mass the way the priests usually celebrate Mass. When they had the confession, they first read from a book. After that, they went to kneel in front of the altar, but there was no god. There was a picture of God, but it was just a picture. There was just a tiny cross on the center of the altar.

Well, when they were kneeling in front of the altar they were lined up to be given the host in their right hands. And then they, themselves, swallowed the host. But everyone in the church took communion. Their sins were taken away just by reading in the book. When they had swallowed the host, then they were lined up to be given one swallow of wine apiece from the chalice, probably to wash down the host. In the middle of the prayers, too, they collected money the way the priests always do, but when the priest took it, he showed the money on high to Our Lord (Laughlin, 1980: 19).

We attended the annual meeting of the American Anthropological Association.

ROMIN:

They were telling about all the things that they saw where they worked and what kind of work they went to do in each country. But some of the ones who were gathered there were listening to each other, about each one's work, but others were just having a good time there. Some had taken trips to wherever they wanted in California.

1958 Navenchauc, Zinacantec musicians (Tzotzil)

As for us, after the meeting was over, they served liquor. But it didn't matter who wanted to drink, it made no difference. Let them grab their own drinks, it didn't matter. As for us, we kept looking for liquor after it had run out. We searched and searched from floor to floor, but after it had run out you couldn't find it anywhere, because after it had run out everybody was going crazy looking for it. They were searching in every room, but you couldn't find it anywhere, because there were too many people. That's why the drinks ran out (Laughlin, 1980: 39–40).

ANSELMO:

We returned to the place where the meeting was held, because they were still having a good fiesta there, and all the anthropologists danced.

We got drunk because we drank everything they gave us. The drinks we drank—there were white ones, there were black ones, there were yellow ones! (Laughlin, 1980: 102).

These two Tzotzils who, by chance, watched Ruby shoot Oswald on television, who got lost on the New York subway, marched on the Pentagon, and

commented astutely on automation and race prejudice, hardly seem like the figures in the accompanying photographs. But upon their return, little time passed before both could be seen in all their ritual finery, first as stewards and cantors, then as ensign bearers, with high-backed sandals, red knee socks, green velveteen britches, blue cloaks, red turbans, and black felt hats each topped by a peacock feather (conveniently acquired at the National Zoo in Washington).

It is easy to forget that these faces, these people we look at, are also looking at us.

Bibliography

Espinosa, Luis
1912 Rastros de Sangre. Mexico City.
Laughlin, Robert M.
1976 Of Wonders Wild and New: Dreams from Zinacantán. Smithsonian Contributions to Anthropology, 22. Washington, D.C.
1977 Of Cabbages and Kings: Tales from Zinacantán. Smithsonian Contributions to Anthropology, 23. Washington, D.C.
1980 Of Shoes and Ships and Sealing Wax: Sundries from Zinacantán. Smithsonian Contributions to Anthropology, 25. Washington, D.C.

Author's note: I am indebted to Jan de Vos for providing many fresh insights on the history of Chiapas.

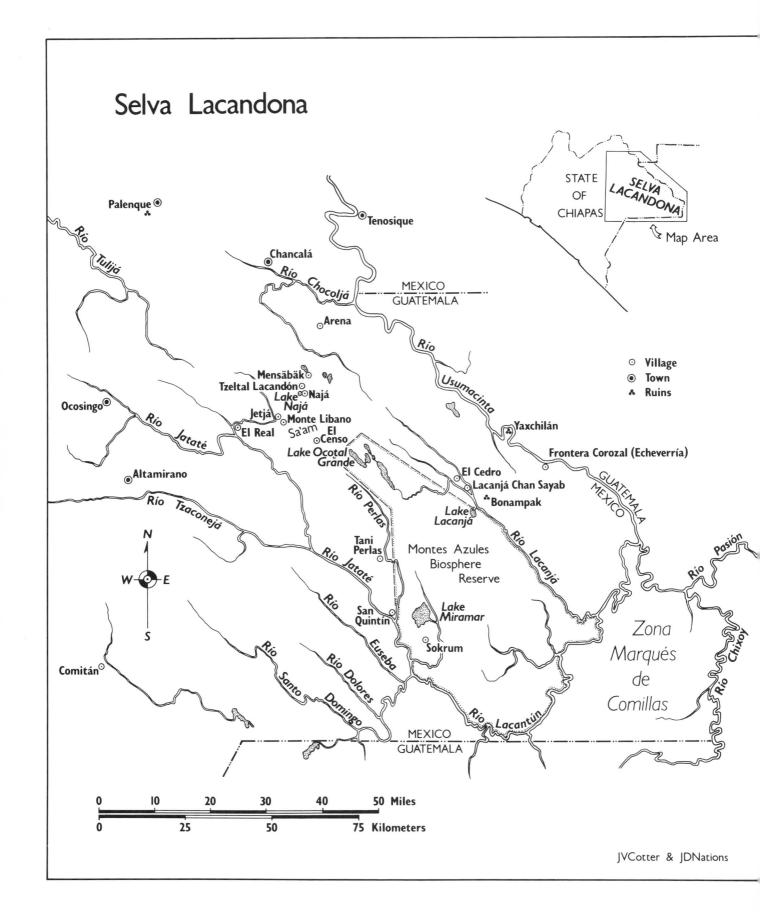

Selva Lacandona

STATE
OF
CHIAPAS

SELVA LACANDONA

Map Area

Palenque

Tenosique

Río Tulijá

Chancalá

Río Chocoljá

MEXICO
GUATEMALA

Arena

Río

⊙ Village
◉ Town
♣ Ruins

Mensäbäk
Tzeltal Lacandón
Lake
Najá
Najá

Usumacinta

Ocosingo

Río Jataté

Jetjá
Monte Libano
El Real
Sa'am
El
Censo

Lake Ocotal
Grande

Yaxchilán

Frontera Corozal (Echeverría)

GUATEMALA
MEXICO

El Cedro
Lacanjá Chan Sayab

Bonampak

Altamirano

Río Tzaconejá

Río Perlas

Lake
Lacanjá

Río Lacanjá

Río Pasión

N

W E

S

Tani
Perlas

Río Jataté

Montes Azules
Biosphere
Reserve

Zona
Marqués
de
Comillas

Río
Euseba

San
Quintín

Lake
Miramar

Sokrum

Río Chixoy

Comitán

Río
Santo

Río
Dolores

Domingo

MEXICO
GUATEMALA

Río Lacantún

| 0 | 10 | 20 | 30 | 40 | 50 Miles |

| 0 | 25 | 50 | 75 Kilometers |

JVCotter & JDNations

The Lacandones, Gertrude Blom, and the Selva Lacandona

James D. Nations

When Frans Blom and Gertrude Duby Blom journeyed on muleback through the Lacandon jungle of eastern Chiapas, Mexico, in 1943, they explored a region blanketed by more than thirteen thousand square kilometers of virgin tropical rainforest. At the time, the only other people in the area were 250 Lacandon Maya Indians, a handful of mahogany loggers, a few teams of chicle gum gatherers and crocodile hunters, and an incipient trickle of immigrant Tzeltal farmers from the nearby Maya highlands.

Down every jungle trail the couple rode they found wilderness, pristine rivers, and an abundance of rainforest wildlife. Peccaries and pacas dashed across the trails at the sound of the approaching explorers. Flocks of parrots and scarlet macaws flew overhead toward mountains that had not seen outsiders in centuries. A million insects hummed and whined and buzzed. By night, tapirs, jaguars, and kinkajoos roamed the jungle near the expedition's campsites. And as dawn appeared, the forest stretched on forever.

Today, as we recognize the fortieth anniversary of Frans and Trudi's first expedition to the Selva Lacandona, the jungle is an entirely different place. Almost half of the forest has been cleared and burned, and much of the rest has been degraded by loggers, colonists, and ranchers. Thin Brahma cattle search for forage where ceiba trees once arched over jungle waterfalls, and felled mahogany trees weight down logging trucks that ply the region's growing network of asphalt and gravel roads. Bulldozers tear paths through primordial vegetation in an obsessive search for petroleum, and left-over hippies step down from second-class buses to search for magic mushrooms in the debris of the Mayan past.

Once the secret refuge of Mayan heritage, the Selva Lacandona has become the frontier home of more than 150,000 immigrant farmers and 70,000 Guatemalan refugees from a neighbor's bloody war. The only remnants of the rainforest's unviolated expanses persist in a few inaccessible valleys and in the haunting photographs of Gertrude Blom.

The ignorance, greed, and progress of civilization have begun their final round of destruction in the Selva Lacandona. The politician's dream to incorporate the rainforest into the national economy will soon bear fruit on eroded hillsides and in weeded, wasted valleys. Centuries from now, if our own civilization has fallen into ruins like those of the ancient Maya, the rainforest may return. But in the meantime, we must join Gertrude Blom in bearing witness to the dying gasp of the Selva Lacandona and watch its once-rich exuberance fade into the smoke of burning pasture fires.

Still—in the face of all this change—for a short while longer something sacred will remain. Laughter from a late-night Lacandon *balche'* ceremony can still glide through the forest and trace ripples across lakes where the Mayan gods reside. In early morning light a lone Mayan hunter, silent and insignificant on a jungle hillside, can still watch rainfall drip to the molding forest floor from orchids and lianas in the canopy above. And the quick eyes of a hidden Harpy eagle can still search the treetops for an elusive meal of monkey.

Although the deforestation of the Selva Lacandona is too exten-

1943 Monte Líbano (Puná), Pepe Castillo, younger brother of Chan K'in Viejo (*Lacandon*)

sive this time for the area to fully recover, rainforest clearing is nothing new to the region. Part of the selva has been cleared before, during the time of the Classic Maya. In fact, one thousand years ago eastern Chiapas supported more people than it does today.

Archaeologists and historians tell us that during the Classic Maya era (250 A.D. to 900 A.D.), hundreds of thousands of Chol-speaking Maya lived in the Selva Lacandona, elaborating complex systems of religion, writing, astronomy, and commerce and practicing agricultural techniques based on an intimate knowledge of the region's environment. As trade networks and political integration expanded, the Maya built cities of stone and plaster and decorated them with finely crafted carvings and brilliantly painted murals. Today, the decaying stones of Palenque, Yaxchilán, and Bonampak stand as mute testimony to the former grandeur of the Classic Maya in the Selva Lacandona.

Why this civilization faltered and disintegrated in the Chiapas rainforest—as it did elsewhere—is the stuff that archaeologists' careers are made of. All we know is that sometime between 700 and 900 A.D. the population abandoned the stone cities and cere-

monial centers and dispersed throughout the countryside. Gradually, the rainforest crept down the uncleared hillsides to reclaim its borrowed valleys. That the jungle returned at all is certain proof that the Maya had preserved large sections of it for hunting and raw materials and as the dwelling places of the forest gods.

As the rainforest regenerated, the Maya of the Selva Lacandona once again became a forest people. During the centuries that followed the disintegration of Classic Maya civilization, the descendants of the architects and street sweepers of Palenque and Bonampak continued to live in the region—frequently in fortified, thatch-roofed communities built on lands in lakes and rivers. The island villages at Lake Miramar and Lake Ocotal Grande and in the Río Jataté were thriving through a brisk trade in forest products—dyes, feathers, rubber, wild cacao, copal incense—when the Old World invaded the New during the early sixteenth century.

It was in these island communities that the Spaniards found the inhabitants of the Selva Lacandona when they entered the region during the early 1500s. But the Spanish diseases had arrived there first. Traveling trade routes by trail and river, the Old World disorders of smallpox, pulmonary plague, measles, and influenza wiped out families, decimated villages, and left the survivors stunned and disbelieving. In the Selva Lacandona, as elsewhere in the Mayan world, as many as 50 percent of the Conquest-era population may have died before they ever saw a Spaniard.

Then came the conquering heroes, dressed in leather and armor, riding strange animals, carrying the cross and the Mayan future

before them. In the Selva Lacandona, the Chol-speaking descendants of the Classic Maya were happened upon by chance by the Spaniard Alonzo Dávila, in 1530, as he searched the jungle for the path that Hernán Cortés had taken from Mexico to Honduras in 1525. Enticed by the idea of Indian riches, Dávila occupied the island village of Lacam Tun ("Great Rock") in the middle of Lake Miramar, but did so with no resistance, for the village's inhabitants had fled at the approach of the Spanish forces. Finding no gold on the island, Dávila pushed on toward Tenosique on the Río Usumacinta.

During the three decades that followed, the Spaniards left the inhabitants of the Selva Lacandona to themselves and concentrated instead upon exploiting the Mayan peoples of the more hospitable Chiapas highlands. But as disease, malnutrition, and harsh conditions claimed the lives of these Indian workers, the Spaniards again turned their eyes toward the Chiapas jungle.

Although they knew that the unpacified Maya of the Selva Lacandona could be reached only with great difficulty, the Spaniards undertook a program to bring them under colonial control. In a series of military and missionary expeditions that ran from 1559 to 1712, the Spaniards killed, captured, or relocated the majority of the inhabitants of the region. The Spanish New Laws of 1542 had proscribed the enslavement of Indian inhabitants of the New World—except in the case of groups who resisted colonial authority. Conveniently, the Chol of the Chiapas jungle resisted their conquerors' cannons and crossbows and their talk of gods from distant lands. As a result, though battles killed hundreds of the jungle's men, women, and children, several thousand still survived to be put to work for the good of the Spanish god and king. From the Ocosingo Valley the Spaniards removed and relocated hundreds of Tzeltal-speaking families. And from the northern and southern jungle, they removed the Chol-speaking Maya. Relocated by colonial officials into the towns of Palenque, Ocosingo, Tila, Yajalón, Tumbalá, and Salto de Agua, these Indian families labored on sugarcane plantations and cattle *haciendas*, where many of their descendants still live today.

For a while the Spaniards' expeditions left the Selva Lacandona essentially vacant; probably only a few hundred people managed to elude their Old World adversaries and their strange diseases. The families that survived hid in the jungle like stalked forest animals, preserving pieces of the past along with their lives.

But almost as quickly as Spanish armies and zealous friars cleared the jungle of its Chol-speaking inhabitants, other Mayan groups—refugees from occupied territories to the north and west—moved in to fill the vacuum. As this mixed group of refugees—Quejach Maya, Itzá Maya, and other Yucatec-speaking Maya—occupied the region during the seventeenth and eighteenth centuries, they too became known as *Lacandones*, a term the Spaniards had learned at Lake Miramar and subsequently applied to all apostate and non-Christian Indians in the jungle. These immigrant families mixed with the surviving Chol Maya, but—for the most part—they too were relocated by later Spanish expeditions designed to bring the region under religious and economic control.

Then, near the end of the eighteenth century, those refugees who had escaped relocation were joined in the jungle's recesses by Yucatec-speaking families who were fleeing disease and disruption in the Guatemalan Petén, the eastern extension of the same tropical rainforest that covers lowland Chiapas. Moving across the Río Usumacinta to escape capture and Catholicism, these long-haired, barefoot Maya were unaware that they had crossed what would later become an international boundary between Mexico and Guatemala.

By simple chance, the families produced by this gradual blend of Chol- and Yucatec-speaking Maya were secure in their jungle isolation for several decades into the nineteenth century. To avoid diseases or detection from the outside world, these new Lacandones dispersed their settlements in isolated family compounds separated by miles of unoccupied jungle. But they remained connected to one another through intermarriage, a common language, and their traditional gods—a score of them represented by small clay godpots graced with humanlike heads and led by "Our True Lord," Hachäkyum.

Left alone, the Lacandones preserved, perfected, and passed down to their children a detailed knowledge of their rainforest environment and a complex system of food production that was both productive and ecologically sound. But plagued by introduced diseases and by raids and strife among themselves, they probably never numbered more than three hundred individuals during these years of isolation.

The world beyond the forest intruded upon the Lacandones once again during the mid-nineteenth century, when logging teams began to fell mahogany trees along the region's numerous rivers. Using teams of oxen, the loggers dumped the tree trunks into the rivers and floated them through miles of forest toward Tenosique and international markets. To the Lacandones, the logging camps became commercial oases where they could trade meat, tobacco, and bows and arrows for salt, guns, cotton cloth, and—inadvertently—more diseases. As late as the 1930s, lumbermen and itinerant *chicleros* who tapped *chicozapote* trees still constituted the Lacandones' chief contact with the modern world and their primary source of epidemics.

Simultaneous with the first logging camps, during the mid-to-late nineteenth century, the first foreign explorers focused upon the Selva Lacandona. During the 1830s and 1840s, John L. Stephens and Frederick Catherwood marched through the forest in search of ancient cities. They explored the ruins of Palenque and met some Lacandones. In the town of Palenque, a few miles from the ruins, they learned that years before, an Irishman named William Beanham had set off into the jungle to visit the Lacandones and had lived with them for nearly a year. Stephens was told that the man returned from the jungle "naked and emaciated, with his hair and nails long."

After a brief stay in Palenque, Beanham had constructed a hut on a nearby river and was preparing for a longer sojourn among the Lacandones when "at length some boatmen who came to trade with him found him lying in his hammock dead, with his skull split open." As Stephens wrote, "He had escaped the dangers of a journey which no man in that country dared encounter, to die by the hands of an assassin in a moment of fancied security."

Although Beanham's murderers were arrested and later imprisoned in Tenosique, an equally severe injustice was committed on him by the people of Palenque. After Beanham died, they scattered and destroyed the papers and "curiosities" he had collected during his months among the Lacandones. "Thus," Stephens said, "with him died all the fruits of his labours."

During their explorations, Stephens and Catherwood discovered William Beanham's only literary legacy, a stanza ("the rhyme faulty and the spelling bad") written in lead pencil upon a wall in the ruins of Palenque. Even this is now lost to posterity. Nonetheless, this long-dead Irishman was the first ethnographer of the Lacandon Maya, and the destruction of his notes and impressions is a loss for all time.

Explorers Karl Sapper, Teobert Maler, Désiré Charnay, and Alfred Maudslay explored the Selva Lacandona toward the end of the nineteenth century. In 1891, Sapper visited Lacandon settlements in both eastern Chiapas and the Guatemalan Petén, where many families still resided at that time. The Lacandones he encountered there were well aware that contact with outsiders brought new diseases and death; as he wrote, "the single appearance of white men is usually enough to lead them to abandon their old dwelling places."

Seven years later, in 1898, Maler tramped through the Selva Lacandona and marveled at the richness of the forest and at the lives of the people who lived there. He too

1898 Lacandones photographed by Teobert Maler (Courtesy Peabody Museum, Harvard University)

noted the impact that outside contact could have on Lacandon society: "Wherever the Indians are not affected by the Spanish element, food is remarkably abundant. But wherever the people have come under Spanish influence, we have sometimes been unable to obtain a single miserable fish even at a high price."

Someplace in the northern Lacandon selva, Maler took the first known photographs of the Lacandon Maya. In one of them a young man and a boy with long, tangled hair stare across the decades with a furtive primitiveness that Maler described as "wild and leonine." Half a century later, those same half-wild but self-possessed eyes would dominate some of the Lacandon portraits taken by Gertrude Blom.

A few years after Maler, Alfred M. Tozzer—"Don Alplelo," the Lacandones called him—appeared in the Chiapas jungle, speaking the Yucatec he had learned in the Yucatán Peninsula and seeking information on all aspects of Lacandon

society. Between 1902 and 1905, long before Bronislaw Malinowski—the purported father of anthropological fieldwork—had introduced himself to the Trobriand Islanders, Tozzer was living in palm-thatched huts, interviewing Lacandones in their own language. He was the first, and perhaps the finest, of a dozen professionally trained anthropologists who would work with the Lacandones over the following eighty years. He grew his hair long, ate monkeys, and kneeled beside his Lacandon friends as they chanted before flaming godpots. His requests for copies of the godpots to take back home were countered by demands that he first learn the chants and prayers that must accompany them. He apparently did so, for the godpots the Lacandones gave him are displayed today in Harvard University's Peabody Museum.

One of Tozzer's primary Lacandon informants was José Bor García, father of Chan K'in Viejo, the patriarch and religious leader of today's northern Lacandones and a central figure in Frans and Trudi's experience with these people. Linguist Robert Bruce once asked Chan K'in, who was a small boy at the time of Tozzer's work, if he remembered the anthropologist.

"I remember him," Chan K'in replied. "He had cameras and was always scribbling things down in little books." The Lacandones of the time, Chan K'in recounted, considered Tozzer to be "a very good man." Nonetheless, as Bruce later wrote, they "did not understand what cameras were, nor what it was Tozzer was always writing in his books; they didn't know where Tozzer had come from, nor why."

Bruce's explanation that the words Tozzer wrote down were still preserved and that he himself had read them brought home to Chan K'in the realization that his own stories and tales could similarly be preserved for future generations. The event was a key factor in the success of Bruce's excellent, ongoing work with Chan K'in Viejo on Lacandon language, religion, and mythology.

Forty years after Tozzer's pioneer research among the Lacandon Maya, Trudi Blom met Chan K'in on a lake in the northern Chiapas jungle and began a friendship that would last for both their lifetimes. The cross-cultural queen and king of the Selva Lacandona, she became the outspoken but loving ambassador of foreign civilization, he the quiet, Zen-like master of the forest.

Trudi and Frans Blom's expedition to the Lacandon rainforest in 1943 was not the only significant event that affected the Lacandones during that decade. The same years also brought the most dramatic change the twentieth century Lacandones had ever seen— the massive invasion of their rainforest territory by colonizing farmers from other regions of Mexico. In a program similar to the United States Homestead Act, thousands of Indian and *mestizo* peasants were exhorted by government agents to move into the Chiapas lowlands in search of land and new lives. Ironically, many of these immigrant families were Tzeltal and Chol Maya, the descendants of the groups who had been forcibly removed from the region by the colonial Spaniards four centuries before.

The *kaho*, "the community dwellers," as the Lacandones

1945 Lake Najá, Chan K'in Viejo in dugout canoe

called the invaders, established colonies throughout the uninhabited rainforest between the Lacandon settlements. They began to clear and burn the forest to raise corn, beans, chilies, squash, coffee, and cattle. Understandably, the Lacandones—who were reluctant to live near even nonrelated members of their own group— were not pleased with these new arrivals. They drew their settlements into tighter patterns, concentrating on the rivers and lakes of the central jungle region.

Unlike the Lacandones, the new immigrants raised pigs and cattle for sale in commercial markets. Such activities—and the sheer number of new people in the region—placed harsh burdens on the rainforest environment. In fact, the immigrants' activities began to eradicate the forest itself. Instead of allowing agricultural plots to regenerate in natural forest, the Tzeltal and Chol Maya seeded their abandoned *milpa* plots in pasture grasses and dedicated the land to beef cattle.

The final blows to the forest began during the 1960s, when the Mexican government began a program of massive road construction aimed at extracting the rest of the jungle's mahogany and tropical cedar trees. These logging roads pierced the core of Lacandon territory and triggered another massive influx of colonizing farm families. As this second wave of immigrants ate through the forest, wealthy Mexican cattlemen followed in their wake, buying up the families' cleared plots to create large ranches. Supported by generous bank loans, these colonist-cattlemen joined the state's politicians in envisioning the rainforest as one vast cattle ranch, and they set about turning that vision into reality. Where toucans and tapirs had lived only months before, the ranchers produced beef cattle for export to Villahermosa and Mexico City. More than any other act, it was the introduction of commercial cattle ranching into the Selva Lacandona that spelled the death of traditional Lacandon society and of their rainforest environment.

The in-migration of farmers and cattlemen forced the Lacandones to abandon their isolated family settlements and brought them face to face with the modern world. During previous centuries the Lacandones had learned that by concealing their settlements they could avoid unnecessary contact with outsiders. But techniques acquired in earlier times—milpas and houses hidden behind a wall of jungle, trails that seemed to disappear—proved futile against the onslaught of change during the 1960s. As the region's population exploded, constant contact with outside groups became unavoidable. During the mid-1970s government relocation teams searched out the Lacandon families still living in isolation in the forest and moved them into the existing settlements of Mensäbäk and Najá in the northern jungle and Lacanjá Chan Sayab in the south.

Through no choice of their own, the Lacandones had lost the isolation that, for centuries, had protected their lives and their traditions. The old ways of the Maya, as J. Eric Thompson put it, "melted like snow in the hot rays of technological materialism." Simultaneously, the Lacandones began to lose the rainforest environment that had supported both the old ways and their lives.

Today's adult Lacandones are the transition generation in this dramatic wave of change. Their predecessors lived in a world uninterrupted by radios, airplanes, and chainsaws. Their fathers hunted jaguars with bows and arrows where their children now drive rattling trucks down muddy jungle roads. A Lacandon man in the 1980s may begin his day with a chant as old as the Maya themselves and end it hunched over a battery-powered record player blaring raucous *mariachi* music in a language he does not understand. In a very real sense, the Lacandones of today have inherited both the legacy of the ancient Maya and the dubious gifts of the twentieth century.

We are fortunate that this is the generation of Lacandones that Gertrude Blom has captured in photographs. In watching these people change, we see the effects of our civilization on traditional people throughout the world. In turn, their transformation teaches us lessons about ourselves, for we

1979 Najá, K'ayum Ma'ax with accordion

too are a transition generation. Within our lifetimes we will see cultural changes as rapid and as wrenching as those now overwhelming the Lacandon Maya.

The Lacandones of the future will also be fortunate that Gertrude Blom's photographs exist, for in these images they will find faithful reflections of their past and the initial visions of themselves in the contemporary world. When Trudi began to photograph the Lacandon Maya, men still hunted forest animals as they had for centuries. They continue to hunt today, but they use rifles rather than the bows and arrows of their fathers. Lacandon women still grind corn as they have for centuries, but—except for religious ceremonies—they use aluminum grinders purchased in distant cities. In recent years, some men have cut their hair in Western style and traded their tunics for polyester shirts and pants, but the majority still dress in the traditional white cotton *shikur*, even though the cloth comes from the city. In some settlements, families have exchanged the gods of rain, fire, and forest for the flashlight slide shows of evangelical missionaries. Other families remain hidden within the forest, burning *copal* incense and small rubber figures to the silent Mayan gods.

Modern Lacandones are still divided into two distinct groups, northerners and southerners, so called because of their general location in the Selva Lacandona. Most southerners live today at Lacanjá Chan Sayab, although a few hang on at the older community of San Quintín. Northern Lacandones live on the shore of Lake Najá and near Lake Mensäbäk and in a few isolated family settlements scattered across the northern Selva Lacandona. Counting all the families of both groups, the Lacandones number slightly over four hundred people.

Both northern and southern families speak dialects of the same language, appropriately called "Lacandon," a language that is mutually intelligible with Yucatec Maya proper, as well as with the almost extinct Itzá Maya dialect of the Guatemalan Petén. However, word and accent variations between the northern and southern dialects lead the Lacandones to say that they understand "most, but not all" of the other group's speech. Despite their differences, both groups recognize one another, as well as the Yucatec and Itzá Maya, as *winik* (people), though they retain for themselves the term *hach winik* (the true people).

Lacandon men let their long, black hair fall over the shoulders of their white tunics in a contrast that almost seems invented for photography. Northerners distinguish themselves from southern men by cutting bangs across their foreheads. Southern women leave their hair long and flowing and wear colorful versions of the men's white robes. Northern women pull their hair back in a single braid which they decorate with the yellow breast feathers of the toucan, an exotic rainforest bird. They wear a shorter version of the men's white tunic over a colorful skirt decorated with ribbons. For both men and women, the longer sleeves and hem of the southerners' tunics give outsiders a clue to their origin and provide the source of one of the northern Lacandones' names for their southern relatives—chukuch nok, "the long clothes."

Northern Lacandones have a second name for southerners— "those who kill their brothers," a reference to the feuds and wife-stealing raids that southern Lacandones conducted as recently as the 1950s. A few of these raids struck northern Lacandon families, and northerners have never forgotten them. Even today, older adults will warn one another when a southerner approaches the settlement.

In Najá, I once asked Chan K'in Viejo why some families were still afraid of southerners. "They know why," he answered. "They only stopped killing because there are outsiders in the forest now. If there were no outsiders, I myself would be afraid."

In reality, almost all of the fifty-eight known Lacandon homicides were cases of southerners killing southerners. All but one took place before 1940, and most were based on a need for wives. A quick raid on an isolated settlement could net the attackers the wives and daughters of a man out hunting in the forest. Marched hours through the jungle, the women would soon grind corn and bear children for a new husband, though they would never forget their former lives.

Still, most marriages begin not with violence but with courting, visits to the prospective in-laws, and a bride-price of cloth, rifle cartridges, money, and the bridegroom's promises to work months or years for the chosen woman's parents. A hopeful suitor sits in the home of his prospective mate, smokes cigars with her father, and banters with him in ritualized conversation.

"Will you give me your daughter?"

"You don't want to marry my daughter. She's lazy."

"Then she's like me. I don't work. I'm very lazy."

"You, you're very ambitious in your work."

"No, I'm not. Well, will you give her to me?"

The suitor almost always is rejected the first time he asks for the girl. The father tells him, "Come back when your soul is clear and we will talk again." If the young man is serious, he will return in a few weeks to ask his question again.

It is a time of great social stress for the groom-to-be, but marriage is important. A man or woman must have a partner to have children; she must have a husband to obtain corn to eat, and he must have someone to prepare and cook the corn he grows. More than this, both men and women know that when the world ends, all Lacandones will gather at the ruins of the ancient Mayan city of Yaxchilán on the Río Usumacinta. There, the Mayan gods will decapitate those who are unmarried and will hang them up by their heels. They will drain their blood into clay cups and use it to paint the walls of the sacred city that surrounds them.

Like their northern neighbors,

southern Lacandones take several wives if they can find them and afford them and, as one exhausted Lacandon once told me, if they can keep them content. "It takes a strong man to keep three women happy," he said. Southern men soften the problem of strife between co-wives by marrying several sisters. Other men solve the problem by taking as their second wife a girl of eight or ten years of age. Lacandon girls are considered eligible for marriage when they can grind corn and make tortillas—tasks that most girls master by the age of eight. A child bride serves her elder co-wife as firewood gatherer, assistant cook, and live-in baby sitter until she reaches puberty, when the husband turns his favors to her and the older wife must learn to sleep alone again.

Although many northern and southern Lacandon traditions are similar, it is religion that most differentiates the two groups. Religious beliefs in north and south had always varied, but southerners abandoned the traditional Mayan gods during the first half of the century, when their leader died in a devastating yellow fever epidemic and his successors failed to effect a smooth transition in the chaos that followed. In 1957, an American Bible translator set up camp among the southerners after thirteen futile years of missionary work aimed at converting the northern Lacandones of Najá. His efforts among the disoriented southerners were rewarded by the mass conversion of almost all the families at Lacanjá.

Today, southern Lacandones sing Baptist songs in a cane-sided hut with a laminated roof. Two long-haired Lacandon men sit behind a makeshift pulpit as elders, examining songbooks they cannot read. Without warning, they stand and begin singing hymns translated from English into Lacandon. One by one, the congregation gradually joins in, each person beginning with the song's first notes, to create a quiet cacophony that never drowns out the songs of the jungle insects outside. When the white man stands to preach about a jealous God from a distant land, the young men on the back bench joke and poke at one another and a fat woman surrounded by children repeats the preacher's phrases in a dialogue of ancient ways and new religion.

Recent missionary efforts have made inroads among the northern Lacandones as well. During the mid-1970s, a visit by a Yucatec-speaking Mayan from northern Yucatán came shortly after the death of the Mensäbäk leader's only son. The missionary exhorted the men to reject their old religion. "Give up your gods and devil worship and your children will not perish," he promised. In the same breath, he promised a gasoline-powered electric generator, a road, and visits by a doctor. The settlement's leader accepted the promises in a move of mourning tempered with greed. Most of the settlement followed, though a few families slipped into the jungle to resume their chants and prayers. Today in Mensäbäk, a Seventh-Day Adventist church graces the tallest hill in the community, and the children sing "Jesus Loves Me" in Lacandon. They scoff at the children of families who have not converted and call their parents "animals in the forest."

At night the men gather around their radios, listening to evangelical broadcasts in Spanish. They garner strength from hearing the word *Jesucristo* sent to them from so far away. They switch from station to station, sometimes listening for hours, sometimes satisfied simply to hear the new god's name and know that tonight, all around the world, others are also expecting Jesus on the next bush plane.

Only a few isolated families and the northern Lacandones of Najá maintain the traditional Mayan religion. Led by Chan K'in Viejo, they have resisted both missionary efforts and the temptations of the technological world. When someone falls ill or when it is time to pay the gods with *balche*, a mildly intoxicating drink made of tree bark and the fermented juice of sugarcane, they lift clay godpots down from the sacred shelf of the godhouse and place them gently on mahogany boards covered with fresh-cut palm fronds. Chan K'in begins to chant in a resonant voice, accusing, promising, offering to pay the gods with incense and small human figures molded of rubber from trees in his garden plot. He leans over the tiny rubber figures and whispers, "Wake up, wake up." Then he places them on flaming copal incense in the godpots to be consumed by the gods and carried to the afterlife to pat out the gods' tortillas and serve them food and corn gruel.

Morality is of utmost importance in Lacandon religion. "Both Hachäkyum, Our Great Lord, and Kisin, the Devil, watch over us while we're alive," Chan K'in says. "If you lie, commit incest, murder, or are selfish, Hachäkyum will send fever to kill you, to punish you. Then you must pray and promise gifts of copal incense. If you offer incense, in the morning your fever will be gone."

1970 Najá, Chan K'in Viejo leading *balche'* ceremony

Too wise to discount the successes of modern medicine, he also says, "If a doctor is close, I will go to the doctor and pay him to be cured. But I will also go to Hachäkyum and give my prayers to him."

I once watched Chan K'in stand up from an ongoing curing chant, walk outside the godhouse to accept an injection from a visiting Mexican physician, then return to his prayers to Hachäkyum, his chant stronger than ever and his godpots still blazing with copal.

The gods cure, protect, and punish and also remind the Lacandones of their proper place in nature: Känänk'ash, Lord of the Forest, K'ak', the Lord of Fire, Mensäbäk, Maker of Black Rain Powder and Harbinger of Death. They live on sacred lakes in caves filled with the bones of ancient leaders and with godpots overflowing with burned incense. To supplicate the gods, the men periodically make long pilgrimages to the holy cities of Yaxchilán and Palenque, where they chant and search for small stones to place inside their godpots so the gods will come and sit within the godhouse and listen to their prayers.

On other occasions, the women must prepare *tamales* from the meat of monkeys, the Mayan gods' favorite food. Small pieces are placed in the mouths on the heads of each diety's godpot. The men roll cigars of home-grown tobacco and place them on the godpots' lips. Newly harvested crops from the garden plot must similarly be offered to the gods before the families themselves can enjoy them.

I offer you the first fruits of my corn, Känänk'ash, Lord of the Forest. It comes from the virgin cornfield. It is for my daughter, it is for my wife, it is for my first-born son.

I am giving you its essence. I am also eager to eat it. Take it and eat it, then I myself will have some.

I won't cut your trees again until another green year comes. I am giving you their essence. I will not bother you for another year. I am through bothering you for another year.

During lighter moments, Chan K'in will tell you of the creation of human beings and the animals in the forest. Ask him for a story after dinner and he clicks his false teeth, glances at you from the side of his eyes, and launches into the story of the rabbit who fooled the jaguar, mimicking the animals' voices and pausing just long enough for his young sons to laugh. He is the grandfather of us all, the gray-haired wizard of the forest, watching the world through the smiling eyes of a man who climbs mountains and winds down jungle trails with the facility of a much younger man.

In the Lacandones' world of change, men with flowing hair climb into helicopters and fly above the forest to meetings with government officials. Young boys in tunics and plastic shoes talk of plans to have a car and a girlfriend in the capital city.

In the midst of these distortions, Chan K'in Viejo kneels in his godhouse, singing to the gods of lakes and forest, listening to their answers in the wind, watching ripples on the lake. Never defiant or haughty, he nonetheless resists the distractions of the mechanical world that is bulldozing its way into the jungle to steal its trees and children. He rejects the spurious arguments of timber agent and converted Lacandon alike.

"I have watched the Lacandones who have given up their gods. They sit and look at paper they say was written on by their Lord. But they never look up to see the works of Hachäkyum—the sun, the stars, the sky."

As long as Chan K'in lives, he and his nephews, nieces, cousins, sons, and daughters will remain as Gertrude Blom once described all the Lacandones: "They are free men . . . and they feel equal to any other human being."

Thirty years after Gertrude Blom's first trip to the Selva Lacandona, I stood on the mud and grass airstrip in the Lacandon settlement of Mensäbäk and watched a Cessna bush plane bounce to a halt before a group of thirty Lacandon Maya men and women. The Lacandones waited motionless while three Mexican businessmen emerged from the plane like space travelers from a time warp. Standing at the edge of the rainforest, with bare feet and white cotton tunics, the Lacandones looked more like figures from a lost Maya codex than they did a reception committee on a jungle airstrip.

After the businessmen had perfunctorily greeted the Lacandones, a buxom young woman in high heels and polyester dress stepped down from the plane and began snapping photos with an Instamatic camera. The businessmen pulled bolts of cheap cotton cloth from the plane and tore them into sections to hand out to the Lacandon women. Then, amid all the hubbub, they lifted thick documents from a briefcase. None of the Lacandones could read and only a few spoke Spanish, and so no time was wasted on fine print or negotiations. After the Mexicans' hurried explanation, the Lacandon men lined up and eagerly affixed their thumbprints to the contracts. The conference completed, the group piled back into the plane and took off for the settlements of Najá and Lacanjá, where they would repeat the scene and close two more deals.

Twelve months later, with legal contracts filed, the government-owned logging company that the businessmen represented bulldozed roads toward the Lacandon communities and began to rattle the hills with chain saws and falling trees. During the months that followed they extracted thousands of mahogany, tropical cedar, and ceiba trees from Lacandon lands. According to the foreman of one logging team, in a single period of twenty days his group wrenched two million dollars worth of logs from the Lacandon rainforest. The Lacandones grasped the full meaning of the contracts they had signed when workmen began to log the hillsides at the edge of their settlements.

Not all the Lacandones had been so quickly duped into selling their rainforest heritage. Asked by government officials to sign the logging contracts, Chan K'in Viejo advised them that the jungle's mahogany trees weren't his to sell. "I didn't plant the trees," he said. "They're God's," meaning Hachäkyum, the major Lacandon deity. "Go ask Him."

But of course they didn't. Instead, through a suspect political manipulation, government agents appointed the old man's son the *presidente* of the Najá settlement and obtained his signature in exchange for a truck and a headful of promises.

As payment for Hachäkyum's trees, the Lacandones received periodic cash settlements and assurances of unseen deposits to a community fund in the state capital. They used the cash to buy medicines, kerosene, .22 caliber rifles, radios, battery-powered record players, and wristwatches. The community funds went to government-designed "development projects," the most visible of which was the installation of a CONASUPO supermarket in each of the three major Lacandon settlements. In the stores families could purchase such incongruous items as cookies, refined sugar, white flour, chewing gum, canned fruit juices, honey, and packaged ground corn. An engineer charged with easing the Lacandones' introduction into the world of commercial supermarkets told me, "We must teach these people how to live."

Within a year the stores' periodic resupply network had faltered, then ceased altogether. The three stores stood empty—fitting monuments to government bureaucracy and the frustrations of tropical development projects. When I inquired about the program in the state capital, a government official insisted that the seven-million-peso community fund had been totally exhausted; privately, other officials whispered that the fund had never existed.

Watching this greed-fueled destruction of the Lacandon rainforest was my introduction to the problem of tropical deforestation. It took me no time to learn that the Selva Lacandona was only a small part of a much larger process of destruction—a process that threatens to eliminate most of the world's tropical rainforest and rainforest peoples, as well as one million of our planet's animal and plant species, before the turn of the century.

Throughout the world, some one hundred thousand square kilometers of tropical rainforest are cleared and burned each year in the name of survival, progress, and profits, and another one hundred thousand square kilometers are degraded by logging, fires, and livestock grazing. The repercussions of this act, says Harvard researcher Edward O. Wilson, will be worse than "energy depletion, economic collapse, limited nuclear war or conquest by a totalitarian government. It is the folly which our descendants are least likely to forgive."

Ironically, we know very little about what we are destroying. Only one out of six tropical organisms has been described and named by scientists. The world's remaining rainforests hide twice as many unknown species as scientists have examined and classified since Linnaeus began the process 230 years ago.

The prospects of what we stand to lose through this mindless destruction are awesome. Walk into your local pharmacy to have a prescription filled, and chances are one in two that the substance the pharmacist hands you is derived from a wild plant or animal. Chances are one in four or five that the original ingredients came

from a tropical rainforest. One of the best-known examples is the barbasco vine, *Dioscrorea composita*. Three decades ago the barbasco vine was known only as a jungle fish poison used by Indians—including the Lacandones—in Mexico and Central America. Today it is one of the world's primary sources of diosgenin, the active ingredient in birth control pills.

Harvard botanist Richard Evans Schultes has identified more than thirteen hundred plant species utilized by Indians of northwest Amazonia as medicines, poisons, or narcotics. One such discovery by a previous researcher led to the use of tubocurarine as a muscle relaxant during surgery. Better known by its Amazonian name, *curare*, tubocurarine is used by Indian tribes to poison arrow points. Western surgeons use it to temporarily paralyze the heart and lungs during open heart surgery. The plant's active alkaloid has now been synthesized, but the natural rainforest product still provides the standard for its use.

Medical researchers now appreciate the fact that tropical rainforests are the world's most prolific source of alkaloid-producing plants. Rainforest-derived alkaloids already are in use against leukemia and cardiac disease, and they show promise in combating hypertension and tumorous cancer. Schultes found that in the ten years prior to 1979 researchers had isolated 278 new alkaloids from Amazonian rainforest plants alone. In short, he said, the world's tropical rainforests are "a veritable, almost limitless, chemical factory—and a chemical factory almost untouched, waiting for the attention of scientific research."

During the summer of 1983 a

Lacandon man showed me a large bean pod growing on a bush by his house. "This cures rabies in dogs," he said, and he proceeded to give me the recipe—four beans from this bush and some bark from the *akum te* tree, mixed with regular black beans from the kitchen. "Feed this to a dog with rabies and he'll get well," he said. "There are lots of curing plants here in the jungle."

Another great promise of the rainforest lies in the field of pest control. In response to the rainforest's great diversity of species and the astronomical number of jungle insects, rainforest plants produce an enormous array of repellent chemicals. The constant need to develop new agricultural pesticides has led investigators to, for example, the New World genus *Lonchocarpus*. Trees of this genus produce a natural insecticide of great economic interest to farmers. Interestingly, Lacandones use the bark of one of the species of the tree for another purpose. It serves as the primary flavoring in the traditional religious drink, *balche'*.

Lacandones also use the powdered bark and sticky sap of the *tsayok* tree, *Aspidosperma megalocarpon*, to kill cockroaches. House beams made from the tree will hold down cockroach populations by releasing chemicals that go unnoticed by humans but which are deadly to roaches. And small blobs of the sap daubed on the ropes that dangle foodstuffs from the ceiling will keep the roaches from eating your lunch.

The reasons for conserving the world's tropical rainforests go on and on. Some of the best are economic—new medicines, food crops, industrial fibers, gums,

spices, dyes, resins, oils, lumber, cellulose, and wood biomass. In purely economic terms, destroying the world's tropical rainforests drives up the cost of almost everything else. "As the planet becomes simpler biologically," writes Thomas Lovejoy of the World Wildlife Fund—United States, "it becomes more expensive economically: fish are smaller and dearer; lumber is narrower, shorter and more expensive." In sum, says Lovejoy, "dwindling natural resources fuel inflation."

On the other hand, some of the reasons for rainforest conservation are ethical or aesthetic. Ecologically conscious individuals usually require only one argument about why we should preserve large sections of the world's tropical rainforests: rainforests have enriched the earth for over one hundred million years, they are the cradle of terrestrial evolution, and they are "the richest and most exuberant expression of life on land," as ecologist Lawrence Hamilton has noted. As the home of almost half of the earth's plant and animal species, rainforests form a crucial element in our global ecosystem. Rainforests and the species that inhabit them have as much right to exist as humans do.

Unfortunately, ethical and aesthetic arguments usually fall on deaf ears. Economic arguments find a more receptive audience, but they too may go unheeded, sometimes because of our hubris, sometimes because the pressing needs of survival prevent people from thinking beyond tomorrow. And in other cases, individuals find that they can make a fast buck by logging, clearing, and burning the rainforest, and care little if it is at the expense of the rest of the world. An expatriate American cat-

tle rancher told Robin Hanbury-Tenison in the Brazilian Amazon, "You can buy the land out there now for the same price as a couple of bottles of beer per acre. When you've got half a million acres and 20,000 head of cattle, you can leave the lousy place and go live in Paris, Hawaii, Switzerland, or anywhere you choose."

Faced with such arrogance and greed, we may find that, rather than threats of species extinction or spiritual impoverishment, it will take the grim repercussions of tropical deforestation—flooding, erosion, siltation of rivers and lakes, decreased rainfall—to force humankind to pay attention to the plight of the jungle. We may not have to wait long. These repercussions have already begun, and in a few places, decision-makers are being forced to take heed.

Unfortunately, Mexico is not one of those places. Having destroyed 80 percent of the nation's tropical rainforest, the banks, the government, and the people have dedicated themselves to eradicating the final six thousand square kilometers of the Selva Lacandona. In a defiant act of ignorance the Mexican government is now embarked on the Plan Chiapas, a regional development program touted as a strategy "to consolidate the territorial integration of the rainforest and reaffirm its insertion into national development." In effect, though, the plan is nothing more than the same wolf in a new cowhide—a strategy to increase rainforest clearing and cattle production in an area ill-suited for these activities.

The plan's project description paints a clear picture. The goals of the Plan Chiapas, it states, are to take advantage of the agricultural and livestock potential of the remaining rainforest by extending the agricultural frontier, increasing the production of basic grains, and helping achieve self-sufficiency of food production in Mexico. One corollary of the plan calls for sending twenty-six thousand farm families into the Marqués de Comillas, the small elbow of Chiapas rainforest that juts into Guatemala in the easternmost extension of the state. It is the last large block of virgin rainforest in Mexico.

Confronted with this fact, an official from the Ministry of Agrarian Reform in the state capital declared that sacrificing the rainforest of the Marqués de Comillas would preserve other areas of the Selva Lacandona by giving the colonizing families a home—a comment reminiscent of what the United States army major said about a small village in Viet Nam: "We had to destroy Ben Tre in order to save it."

Then, too, the Plan Chiapas provides an economic cover for the new military road that is the plan's central feature. Called the "Southern Frontier Highway," the road will link the Marqués de Comillas with Palenque and San Cristóbal by bulldozing a path parallel to the Río Usumacinta and the Guatemalan border below the Río Lacantún. The goal here, the plan states, is "improved vigilance of the southern frontier." This is the region currently inhabited by tens of thousands of Guatemalan refugees who have fled across the border into Chiapas to escape the genocidal, anti-Communist campaigns of Guatemalan presidents Lucas García and Ríos Montt. Since this is also perhaps the richest oil-producing region of Mexico, security here is a major concern for the government, and the construction, already underway, would be difficult to halt.

Aware that the Plan Chiapas is the death sentence of the Selva Lacandona, government agents have thrown a sop to Mexico's conservationists in the form of a five-year pilot project on ecological development. The project will be carried out by the Instituto Nacional de Investigaciones Sobre Recursos Bióticos (INIREB), a tropical research organization staffed by some of Mexico's foremost ecologists, biologists, and agronomists. This group of dedicated researchers is charged with finding and evaluating ecologically sound systems of natural resource production in the rainforest biome. That they must do this in the bulldozer's wake adds an especially urgent aspect to this formidable task.

One of the most promising ecological wonders they will encounter in the Selva Lacandona is the traditional farming system of the Lacandon Maya. The system is practiced today by only a few families—those who have slipped further into the forest as modern Mexico has approached, away from the lumber roads and machines, away from the new foods and *mariachi* music. With tapirs and howler monkeys for neighbors, these families have continued an agricultural tradition that sustained their ancestors for centuries. They live there unobtrusively, as though they were waiting for the outside world to seek out their knowledge.

I've visited one of these farmers, José Camino Viejo of Mensäbäk, yearly since 1974. He is one of the finest tropical farmers in the Americas and a reminder of the agricultural sophistication achieved by native peoples before contact with western civilization. He lives with his wife in an isolated compound hidden in the

forest, in an echo of the settlement pattern that all Lacandones once followed. The half hour's walk to his house takes you away from the main settlement at Mensäbäk, through regrowing milpas past a trail that is left overgrown and seemingly abandoned. But a short distance down that trail you come to the outer edge of José Camino's agronomic paradise, an island of food and raw materials in a backwater of weeds and cattle and regrowth.

As if in defiance of the politician's declarations that traditional agriculture is obsolete and wasteful, José has farmed the same three-hectare plot (about seven acres) for the past twelve years. A quick survey in 1976 revealed seventy-nine different species of food and fiber crops growing in a single hectare. Light years beyond the Mayanists' holy trinity of corn, beans, and squash, he harvests rice, pineapples, sugarcane, bananas, taro, manioc, yams, limes, spices, oranges, cotton, avocados, rubber, cacao, and pounds and pounds of tobacco, the Lacandones' traditional cash crop, formerly sold to itinerant muleteers who transported the prized leaves to market in Ocosingo.

The milpa is kept absolutely weed-free; on his daily patrols to examine his crops, José cuts out uninvited plants as quickly as they sprout, leaving only those that he recognizes as valuable natural species, like wild pineapple, wild dogbane, or breadnut *ramón*. Planting two corn crops per year, if he chooses, José can harvest up to five tons of shelled corn per hectare and an equal amount of root and vegetable crops. By contrast, nearby cattle ranches—during the seven to ten years they produce before being abandoned—achieve twenty-two pounds of beef per hectare per year, and they leave behind a wasteland rather than a regenerating tropical forest.

Not far from her husband's milpa, José's wife, Koh, washes their cotton tunics in a small lake they share with a single crocodile. "Poor crocodile," he once told me. "I would never kill it."

Unlike many modern Lacandones, José eschews contact with jungle colonists and airstrip tourists. And he laments the destruction of the rainforest in a voice that is calm and quiet and sane: "The outsiders come into the jungle and they cut the mahogany and kill the birds and burn everything. Then they bring in cattle, and the cattle eat the jungle. I think they hate the forest. I just plant my crops and weed them, and I watch the birds and I watch the forest to know when to plant my corn. When the mahogany flowers fall in the spring, I seed the corn and wait for the rains to come. As for me, I guard the forest."

Properly researched and adapted, aspects of the Lacandones' traditional knowledge of tropical agriculture could be offered to immigrant colonists who enter the forest from other kinds of ecosystems and who end up burning and destroying the jungle in their attempts to make it produce.

Providing new systems of food production to families in the Selva Lacandona is only one of the potential solutions to the destruction of the rainforest. Intensifying beef cattle production—but only on land already cleared—is another. Both of these solutions will require years of hard work, both scientific and political. In the meantime, the best way to preserve pieces of the Selva Lacandona is to set them aside as parks and wildlife reserves.

This idea has been at the core of Gertrude Blom's writings and speeches since she came to know the jungle. As early as the 1950s, she and Frans were writing letters and proposals to government leaders, urging the creation of a system of national parks in the Selva Lacandona.

Under pressure from Trudi and other conservationists, in 1978 the Mexican government announced a presidential decree setting aside 3,312 square kilometers of the Selva Lacandona as a biosphere reserve under the aegis of the Man and the Biosphere Program of UNESCO. Called the Montes Azules Biosphere Reserve, the region encompasses the south-central section of the Selva Lacandona and includes Lake Miramar, the Ocotal lakes, and the Lacandon settlement of Lacanjá Chan Sayab. First defined in 1968, biosphere reserves are designed to safeguard genetic resources and preserve endangered species. They do this by incorporating these resources and species, as well as existing human populations, into a multiple-use program that conserves ecosystems without prohibiting their use for human benefit. According to the official decree, cattle ranching and agriculture are permitted within the limits of the reserve only on "land already cleared and on land fallowed for fewer than 20 years."

Conservationists around the world applauded this enlightened policy of rainforest conservation. They were sobered by the 1982 report of Rudolfo Lobato, a member of a Mexican-German research team, who noted that "none of the activities or proposed objectives of the decree have been carried out, nor has the reserve been delineated." According to the research team, the Montes Azules Biosphere Reserve is a reserve on paper only. On the ground, colonists and cattlemen continue to clear and burn the reserve's rainforest at the rate of twenty square kilometers per year. The research team also noted that the failure to protect the reserve can be traced to the "lack of a political decision" to appropriate the funds necessary to turn it into reality.

The researchers then noted that "it is not possible to think that the pattern of destruction will halt in the future." Instead, intentional clearing and accidental burning will continue because increasing numbers of slash-and-burn farmers enter the reserve each year and because the amount of land these families clear is increasing, owing to their emphasis on cattle ranching rather than on food production.

Finally, Lobato's study of Montes Azules pointed out that the ongoing construction of roads and other infrastructure for oil exploration "will bring in increasing amounts of colonization and increasing destruction." In sum, he stated, "the total area of the Lacandon rainforest will be disturbed, leaving only small islands of virgin areas." The areas cited for possible survival comprise only 10 percent of the proposed Montes Azules territory—the most inaccessible regions. More than half of the reserve, the report said, has been officially designated as "areas for future colonization."

The words of the Montes Azules research team mirror those of Trudi and Frans in a 1959 proposal to create a rainforest park around the archaeological ruins of Yaxchilán, on the Río Usumacinta: "In only a few years, this great rainforest will be covered with a network of roads, camps, and new population centers. And then will come the destruction of this great and beautiful jungle; the wild animals will disappear, and the mahoganies and giant cedars and now-rich and fertile land will become sterile."

Despite this grim assessment, some glimmers of hope remain. Under the guidance of Mexico's foremost conservationists, the presidency of Miguel de la Madrid has created a new Ministry of Urban Development and Ecology, with a Subsecretary of Ecology. The agency is headed by scientists who are vitally interested in preserving sections of the Selva Lacandona, especially the Montes Azules Biosphere Reserve. In conjunction with researchers from INIREB, they have announced plans for a resurgence of forces to halt destruction within the reserve and for its expansion from 331,200 hectares to one million hectares—a strategic move that would increase the reserve's size by a factor of three. The future of the Montes Azules Biosphere Reserve now stirs in the hands of these concerned individuals, and it is largely up to them to reverse the region's history of senseless devastation.

Meanwhile, the destruction of the Selva Lacandona continues, and Mexico has declared a new national tree: the stump. Still, the rainforest will survive, though perhaps not in great area in Mexico. Across the Río Usumacinta, however, in Guatemala, recent government decrees have created a system of rainforest protection matched in Central America only by Costa Rica, a nation that has set aside 10 percent of its territory as parks or forest reserves. Tropical rainforest will also survive into the twenty-first century in Belize, Pa-

1983 Lacandon jungle between Rancho Cacao and Najá

nama, and Nicaragua, and perhaps in Honduras.

Rainforest will survive in Central America and elsewhere in the world because conservationists like Gertrude Blom remind us daily of the vital importance of these forests and of the folly of destroying them. Through writings, speeches, and photographs, Trudi is the constant voice reminding us of treasures lost and of what we still stand to lose. She is the living conscience of the jungle, bearing witness to destruction and pushing forward with positive alternatives. In the Selva Lacandona the Lacandon people may not always understand the political theory behind Trudi's work, but they understand her goals and they share them, for it is both their home and her dreams that are at stake.

Conservationists must entrust their successes and their strategies to future generations, for we cannot be certain that the wildlife reserves and forest parks of today will not become the lumber yards and cattle ranches of tomorrow. Only through challenges passed on to others can conservationists ensure that their work will continue through the decades. In this, Trudi has never failed. Her success

in inspiring new generations of researchers is her promise that people will still be bearing witness to a better vision of the world long after she and the Lacandones have passed into legend.

Only on rare occasions did my time in a particular Lacandon community coincide with a visit there by Trudi, but when it happened, I always knew in advance. Lacandones anticipate her visits with a mixture of joy and dread.

Landing bush planes filled with outsiders are a common occurrence in Lacandon settlements today, and they rarely generate much excitement anymore. The vacationing adventurer who rents a plane in San Cristóbal to fly into the jungle and live a week among the Lacandones and be adopted into the tribe may soon find himself standing ignored on a mud airstrip, surrounded by no one, while jungle insects echo the buzzing drone of the airplane as it disappears over the mountains.

Not so when Trudi arrives. Children converge on the airstrip as bees converge on a queen. Tiny figures in long hair and tunics, they run to hold her hands and stand beside her. Women lean against their doorways and smile, and the men rush to lift and carry equipment to her campsite. When she arrives on horseback, word passes from Tzeltal village to Chol village down the trail, and Lacandones will be waiting at the river when she emerges from the forest.

To watch her move among the Lacandones is to capture her essence as surely as her photographs capture the essence of the Lacandones. She cajoles them, berates them, chastises them, counsels them, and jokes with them with a sternness tempered with love and a lifetime of shared experiences.

At night, when the campfires are settling into ashes and Trudi's invited travelers are struggling in their hammocks, she and the Lacandones talk into the night, mixing forty years of common understanding with a bewildered awe of the future, creating a pastiche of laughter and unwept tears that they show to no one else.

Once again, Trudi has come home to the jungle and—if only for tonight—Hachäkyum is in his heaven and all is right with the world.

The Photographs

1948 Najá, Lacandon man

1959 Cedro, Lacandon boy

1955 Jungle between Las Margaritas and San Quintín, Tojolabal Indians

1958 Jataté, Vicente Bor planting corn (*Lacandon*)

1955 Santiago, Ladino man on horseback

1959 Romerillo, Chamula women (Tzotzil)

1944 Malinalco, Ladino woman

1964 Lacanjá Chan Sayab, Celestino (*Lacandon*)

54

1963 Amatenango, Tzeltal girls in school

1958 San Cristóbal de las Casas, Zinacantec boys (*Tzotzil*) at political rally for López Mateos

1955 San Bartolomé de los Llanos, Tzotzil musicians at the Festival of San Sebastián

1952 Chamula, In the medical clinic of the National Indian Institute

1958 Zinacantán, Actors during the Festival of San Sebastián (Tzotzil)

1975 Lacandon jungle, Deforestation

1977 Chan K'in Presidente, Mateo Viejo, and K'in García in the highlands (*Lacandon*)

1982 Deforested hillside between El Real and Najá, during the ash fall from the eruption of El Chichonal

1970 Najá, Mateo Viejo leading other Lacandon men

1978 Najá, Lacandon woman making clay figures to sell

1974 Lacandon jungle between Sibál and Najá

1979 Najá, Cut mahogany

1970 Lake Najá, Lacandones in dugout canoe

1954 Najá, Cutting mahogany for dugout canoe (*Lacandon*)

1963 Najá, Chan K'in Viejo with his son, K'in García, in the godhouse (*Lacandon*)

72

1961 Ruins of Lacanjá, K'in Obregon (*Lacandon*)

1975 Lacanjá River

1956 San Andrés, Preparation for the Festival of San Andrés; sacristans building the sacred path (Tzotzil)

1960 San Juan Chamula Carnival, The fire run (Tzotzil)

1962 Santiago, The Saint, San Andrés, visiting at the Festival of Santiago (Tzotzil)

1967 San Miguel Mitontic, Religious procession (*Tzotzil*)

1970 Magdalenas, Festival of Santa Marta (Tzotzil)

1971 Road to Tzontehuitz, the sacred mountain of Chamula, Chamula family (*Tzotzil*)

1974 Santiago, Religious official (Tzotzil)

1946 On the road to San Juan Chamula, Chamula boy carrying burlap bag of pine boughs for a ceremony (*Tzotzil*)

1959 Romerillo, Children watching puppet show (*Tzotzil*)

1953 Ichin Ton, Chamula teacher with Zinacantec students (*Tzotzil*)

1943 Jetjá, Don Florentino with his son (*Tzeltal*)

1961 Tzeltal lowlands, Women and children from migrating community (*Tzeltal*)

1951 Lacandon jungle, Julio, the cook, on expedition

1948 Montería, Mahogany loggers at the Lacanjá River

1948 Lacandon jungle, Frans Blom on expedition near the Lacanjá River

1946 San Quintín, Pedro Contreras with armadillo

1965 Chilil, Cutting hair (Tzotzil)

1952 Huistán, Old man carrying wheat (Tzotzil)

1976 Trudi's camp at Najá, Chan K'in Viejo with his wife Koh (*Lacandon*)

1952 Sivacá, Vicente Bor with Tzeltal school boys

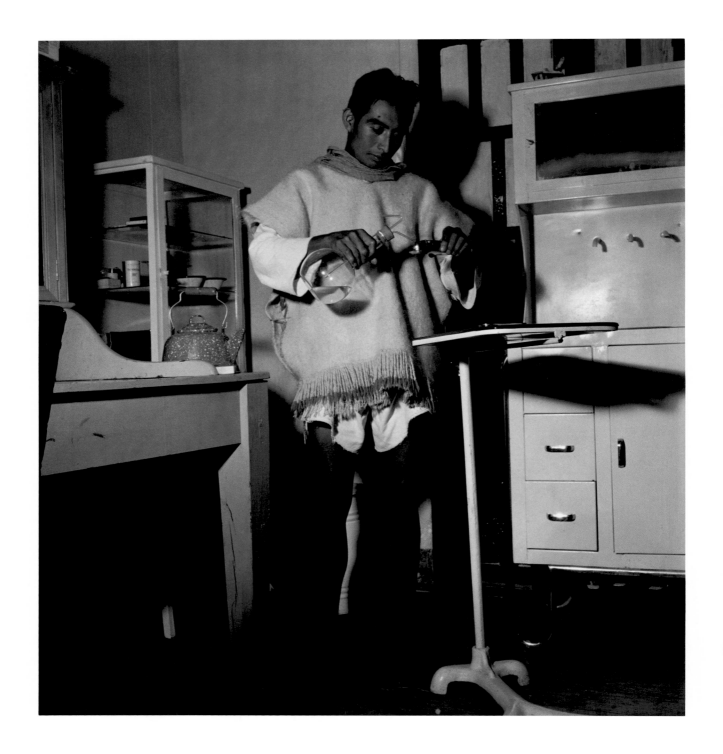

1952 Zinacantán, Zinacantec nurse in the National Indian Institute (Tzotzil)

1952 Najá, Chan K'in Viejo weighing tobacco (*Lacandon*)

1979 San Cristóbal de las Casas, Lacandon men from Lacanjá Chan Sayab visiting Gertrude Blom at Na Bolom

1955 Santiago, Ladino family with Indian maid from Chenalhó (Tzotzil)

104

1941 Yautepec, Zapatista

1941 Yautepec, Zapatistas

1958 San Cristóbal de las Casas, Religious procession in the barrio of San Felipe

1965 San Cristóbal de las Casas, First communion

1959 Najá, Kimbor (*Lacandon*)

1978 Lacanjá River, Jorge K'in and Alfonso Chan K'in (*Lacandon*)

1948 Arena, Lacandon men near the Chocoljá River

112

1974 Najá, Chan K'in Viejo with his oldest wife, Koh, and his son Chan K'in Tercero (*Lacandon*)

1958 Jataté, Pedro K'ayum (*Lacandon*)

1959 El Real, Lacandones from Monte Líbano (Puná)

1967 Yaxchilán, Ceiba, the sacred tree of the Maya

1974 Yaxchilán, Chan K'in Viejo with his son at the temple of Hachäkyum (*Lacandon*)

1977 Najá, K'ayum Ma'ax (*Lacandon*)

1958 Jataté, Pedro K'ayum cutting down ceiba tree with machete (*Lacandon*)

1946 Lacandon jungle, Mahogany workers and the first tractor in the jungle

1960 Chilón

1973 Frontera Corozal, Clearing land

1974 Burning jungle between Ocotal and Cedro

1968 Lacandon jungle near Lacanjá Chan Sayab, Cut mahogany

1972 Huitiupán, Gourd tree

1951 San Cristóbal de las Casas, Calle Diego Dugelay

1952 El Real, Vicente Bor, with sons K'in and K'ayum, leaving the jungle for Na Bolom (*Lacandon*)

1971 Santiago, Captains and patron in festival procession (*Tzotzil*)

1955 San Bartolomé de los Llanos, during the Festival of San Sebastián (Tzotzil)

1959 Santiago, Carrying San Andrés home (*Tzotzil*)

1969 San Miguel Mitontic, Ladino students reenacting Aztec history

1955 San Juan Chamula Carnival, Father Bermudez with festival officials (Tzotzil)

1973 San Miguel Mitontic, Chamula woman praying to San Miguel (Tzotzil)

1954 Chalchihuitán, Chenalhó religious official in the market (Tzotzil)

1961 Yajalón, Tzeltal woman in market

1958 Najá, K'in García in dugout canoe (*Lacandon*)

1948 Censo, Vicente Chaqueta with his son (*Lacandon*)

1978 Lacandon jungle near Tani Perlas

1972 Lacanjá Chan Sayab, K'ayum and Pedro K'ayum (*Lacandon*)

The Jungle Is Burning

Gertrude Blom

Note: This article was originally published in Spanish under the title "Arde la selva, arde" in *Avance* of Villahermosa, Tabasco, and as "Progreso deja ruina biológica en Chiapas" in *El Norte* of Monterrey, Nuevo León. Translation by Laurence Jarosy.

I have been making trips to the Lacandon jungle since 1943. I come from the Swiss Alps, and I fell in love with the jungle from the moment I first saw its incredible vegetation of great trees and exotic plants with leaves as big as parasols, the rare insectlike flowers, the enormous vines that hang from the tops of the trees with roots that curl around the trunks to eventually kill them so that other giant trees can grow in their places.

I was held spellbound by the incredible musical sounds of the insects, from the highest notes to the lowest, and the singing of the frogs and all the hundreds of birds that I had never seen. I listened in amazement to the peculiar cry of the howler monkey and the deafening sound of the tapir crashing through the undergrowth like a tractor. I was transfixed by the enormous flocks of parrots and the macaws describing a rainbow of colors in the sky. Then there were all the snakes of different colors slithering in between the fallen leaves on the floor of the jungle.

I didn't feel any fear in the midst of this new environment; on the contrary I felt quite at home and in my element. I wasn't bothered by the mosquito bites or the bees that were attracted by the smell of sweat or the exhausting heat. I accepted all these little nuisances as part of the fascination of this new environment.

I traveled in this fantastic jungle on long and short expeditions, on mule-back, on foot, and in dugouts. I saw it from the air in its seemingly endless vastness, with its rivers of intense blue and green, its lagoons and lakes of sparkling turquoise, and its turbulent streams.

This jungle filled me with a sense of wonder that has never left me. It has cast a spell over me, and I always return to it; the lumbermen say it is like a Siren.

Everything Is Dying

I have seen all this perish. It started almost imperceptibly—a ranch would appear here and there or a little colony lost somewhere amongst the immense vegetation. The real assault on this rich reserve dates from the 1960s. For more than ten years I have been making annual expeditions to the jungle during the weeks when it is being burned. The purpose of these expeditions is to record in photos and writing the changes that are occurring.

This year we left San Cristóbal by way of Ocosingo and arrived by Lacandon truck at the cattle ranch of El Real. We progressed by mule in the direction of Tani Perlas, the ranch San Bartolo, Lake Ocotal Grande, and afterwards to Infernillo and Najá. It took five long days. Again in truck from Najá we went on to the crossroads of Chancalá, and traveling on a fairly wide road from there we went to the Lacantún River and on to the colony Benemérita de las Americas, which is situated on the right-hand side of the Lacantún River in the area of the Marqués de Comillas.

We visited lumber camps where mahogany was being cut, and on the way we witnessed the riches of the jungle being taken out on huge trailers loaded with enormous tree trunks. This wood is being taken out of a jungle that not so long ago was virgin and completely undisturbed.

From there we left for Yaxchilán,

1983 Burning jungle between El Real and Arroyo Mendez

where we admired some remains of the exquisite Classic Maya culture with its temples and refined architecture and sculptures that have such an incredibly expressive living quality, mute testimonies to a glorious past. The question often comes to mind, What was the reason for the sudden collapse of such a refined culture? The answer is that they too exploited the delicate tropical soil and exhausted it. But it is clear that they did not exploit the jungle half as brutally as we, since they had only stone implements, whereas we have the chain saw and tractor at our disposal. The Maya of that era never burned down huge expanses of jungle for cattle ranching, because they had no cattle.

The jungle was able to recuperate and grow back again. We, with our advanced technology, are condemning it heartlessly to total extinction. Paul and Ana Ehrlich are quite right in saying that if mankind continues abusing the planet as we are today, the effects in the near future will be far worse than the devastation that would be caused by any atomic bomb.

Our expedition, which ended in Palenque, lasted from 4 April to 26 April 1983.

The Banco Rural Is Destroying the Jungle

In 1943 Jethá was a small and barely noticeable clearing in the jungle. Today they are clearing huge stretches of jungle, even on the steep hills; much of the land is being devoured by fires that rage out of control.

Monte Líbano (the old Puná where a few Lacandones once lived scattered in the jungle) today is a large colony, and its inhabitants have cut and cleared an enormous expanse of land. Censo and Tani Perlas used to be virgin forest until a few years ago; now they are densely populated and the forest is being pushed further and further back. Since last year, exactly the same thing is happening at Infernillo.

At Najá, because of the great invasion of people from outside, the Lacandones are also having to move up the hillsides, and they have been forced to group together in communities. They have lost their jungle despite the fact that former president Echeverría granted them land precisely in order to control this outrageous invasion. Now others have usurped what was the best land for their crops, and because of outside influences they have lost the agricultural techniques that they had practiced since time immemorial, methods which were so well adapted to the jungle.

The Tzeltal colony, Lacandon, now has practically no forest at all, and it is the same story in colony after colony until the crossroads of Chancalá-Lacantún, where we traveled on a new road on which enormous works are still taking place. We saw with our own eyes how much of the jungle has been turned into great flat plains, totally denuded of forest.

This is the landscape that one sees over and over again from Palenque right up to Frontera Corozal on the Usumacinta. The destruction is getting worse and worse, not only because of the growing necessity for agricultural land but also because land is being cleared to make way for the introduction of cattle.

Colonies, ranches, *ejidos*, and, I presume, the cattle owners as well, all receive credit from the Banco Rural, an institution which is surprisingly generous. I don't think that any of the representatives of this institution ever actually see how the millions of pesos of credit they give is being spent. If any of them actually took the time to go and see, I'm sure they wouldn't be able to sleep with an easy conscience—unless they are totally unscrupulous and illiterate human beings who haven't bothered to read about the disastrous effects that the hooves of the heavy cattle have on the delicate tropical soil.

Destruction from the Logging of Mahogany

In the 1940s I saw the logging of the mahogany in the region of the Usumacinta River and its tributaries. In those days you didn't hear the deafening roar of the chain saw, which destroys the majestic trees in a matter of minutes; you never smelled the sickly odor of gasoline from the tractors and trailers. Oxen were used to transport the mahogany to the rivers, and the great Usumacinta took the logs to the sea.

They tell me that the machine is a symbol of progress and that it makes the exploitation of timber possible in places where there are no big rivers to transport it. I

1983 Lacandon jungle, The road from Najá to Mensäbäk

don't know if anyone has stopped to think and calculate just how much forest is being lost by the construction of roads and by the clearings left by the tractors when they take the enormous tree trunks out to the road. What is left behind is a terrible biological ruin. They also tell me that these roads mean progress and that they facilitate communication to the colonies. Even where there are no roads, the invasion continues; more and more clearings keep appearing in the jungle.

The *campesino* cuts the jungle to plant his corn so that he can survive; but the first real damage was done by the lumbermen, and the *campesinos* simply follow in their wake. Where there was once virgin forest, there are now scores of invaders cutting down hillsides to make cornfields; and the land they are planting on will soon be barren rock. I ask myself, Who has bothered to take a look at these new settlements? Where are the forest rangers? Trailer after trailer is taking out the last trees and no one says or does anything in protest; it seems that getting rich is more important than the future of our planet. We are leaving a sad legacy for future generations.

In the first days of our expedition a strong storm stopped the burning for a while, but in the end we saw accidental burnings of both cultivated land and virgin forest because firebreaks had not been made. We saw kilometer after kilometer of flames burning wildly and unchecked. It was an apocalyptic vision of the end of the world.

All the way from the Usumacinta to Palenque we were enveloped in a dense cloud of smoke and dust. Everything smelled of burning, and the heat was heavy and asphyxiating. Not even the sun's rays were able to penetrate the curtain of opaque gray smoke in which we were traveling. It was an inferno of destruction.

Never in my forty years of traveling in the jungle had I witnessed such uncontrolled destruction. The sad and painful truth is that *la milpa que camina* (slash-and-burn agriculture practiced on a vast scale) and, even worse, the cattle have subjugated the once majestic jungle.

Cows are being brought into enormous stretches of land, but who knows how long the topsoil is going to support the pasture that these animals feed on? While in these months people don't even have enough corn in other parts of the jungle.

For the poor *campesino* the credit of the Banco Rural is a nightmare. In the Tzeltal colony, Lacandon, they are afraid that they won't be able to cover the repayments and the interest if the cattle get sick. Ten people received five hundred head of cattle, and this has worried the other *ejidatarios* because they are afraid that they are going to lose their land, which they mortgaged to the bank as a guarantee for the repayment of the loans.

The jungle is burning, the great trees are being destroyed, and the land is enveloped in a sinister darkness. No one cares; people seem to be thinking only about the cattle they are going to bring in and the profits from them. They don't stop for a moment to think that the floor of the jungle is turning into laterite, that the springs of water that the cattle need will dry up, that the level of the rivers will go down, that when the rains come, there won't be any plants or trees to stop the water's fury and the rivers will flood the fields and meadows, washing even the houses away in their mighty torrent. Everything will be swept away by the dark muddy water; and the bluish green crystalline rivers will be only a memory.

Is It Worth the Trouble to Write about This Anymore?

I have published many articles which have appeared in newspapers and journals and given many talks on the radio and television. I have taken many photos that show the problem in a much more dramatic way than words ever can, and I have given these to government officials. But now I must ask myself, What is the point in all this effort? It costs me money and a great deal of time and energy, and none of my efforts seem to have wakened people up and made them do something concrete about this disaster.

It is well known what is happening; we are already suffering the terrible consequences of our irresponsibility toward nature. We have upset the ecological equilibrium, and are now experiencing torrential rains, water shortages,

1983 Lacandon jungle, New road from Palenque to Boca de Lacantún

and excessive heat, all because we haven't stopped to appreciate the marvelous environment in which we live. We have only sought to exploit it and have finally exhausted it. And how well we have done it!

We have stood by and allowed all this to happen and haven't looked for solutions to stop or change it; so the situation just gets worse and worse. It is time to stand up and shout before we have no solutions left and our planet becomes a starving and miserable wasteland.

On no account should any more people be allowed to enter and settle in virgin forest. The solution to the problem of the landless *campesino* will not be found in the jungle. Another way must be found, not these short-term solutions that destroy the environment and upset the natural equilibrium. There would be room for more people if they settled in colonies in valleys that have already been deforested. They could be involved in plans and economic projects that would work in harmony with the environment; the deforestation could be controlled and people encouraged to cultivate cocoa, coffee,

and fruit trees. At the same time, small local industries could be started, such as canning factories for the produce. Alligator and *tepezcuintle* (paca) farms could be set up which would provide both food and a source of income for the local population. Small sawmills could be constructed that would utilize the vast quantities of wood thrown by the roadside that now just lie there and rot; this wood could be used to make houses and furniture. These are only a few ideas for solving the problem. First of all, however, all these settlements should be properly studied so we do not create even more problems.

I have personally seen a marvelous project for the planting of cocoa in the area called El Marqués de Comillas. The plan would have been perfect if a little part of virgin jungle had been left intact and if roads hadn't been made through it in a completely haphazard way, since it is along these same roads that all the invaders enter.

It now seems that the Decree of Montes Azules Biosphere is going to be organized. Now is the best time to organize plans for the protection of other places, such as Yaxchilán, Bonampak, the beautiful lakes of Miramar, Ocotal Grande, Lacanjá, Mensäbäk, and Tzibaná, and also the incredible waterfalls of the Santo Domingo River.

I am writing this at the end of April 1983, and I would like to state once more that a vast expanse of the jungle is burning and one of Mexico's greatest riches is being destroyed forever—lost in suffocating smoke and asphyxiating heat. No one is doing anything, and there is a kind of pragmatism around today that says everything for today and let's not

think about some distant future, only the next few years. This kind of mentality will be our downfall.

In the face of the general indifference toward this situation, it is heartbreaking to see the impotence of those who care. Memories of the singing birds, the exquisite colors of the vegetation, and the beautiful rivers come back to my mind like echoes from the past, and the only thing that remains for me to say is that the time has come for us to wake up to what we are doing and take steps to stop the destruction. Let's think about the future or else we are going to be the last species left on this planet.

Exhibitions and Selected Works of Gertrude Duby Blom

Editors' note: For a far more extensive list (1942 to the present) of published photographs, articles, and lectures by Gertrude Blom, please write: Librarian, Biblioteca Fray Bartolomé, Na Bolom, Ave. Vicente Guerrero #33, San Cristóbal de las Casas, Chiapas, México, 29220.

Exhibitions of Photography

1947 Musée D'Ethnographie. Geneva, Switzerland.

1948 Ateneo de Mujeres. Havana, Cuba.

1948 Geografisk Laboratorium. Copenhagen, Denmark.

1949 Asociación Mexicana de Periodistas. Mexico City.

1949 Ateneo de Ciencias y Artes de Chiapas. Tuxtla Gutiérrez, Chiapas.

1952 World Exhibition of Photography. Lucerne, Switzerland.

1961 El Instituto Nacional de Belles Artes. Mexico City.

1961 Museo Nacional de Arte Moderno. Mexico City.

1966 Belles Artes. San Cristóbal de las Casas, Chiapas.

1971 El Instituto Nacional de Belles Artes. Mexico City.

1975 Palacio del Gobierno. Tuxtla Gutiérrez, Chiapas.

1976 Ex-Convento Santo Domingo. San Cristóbal de las Casas, Chiapas.

1978 Ex-Convento Santo Domingo. San Cristóbal de las Casas, Chiapas.

1978 University of Dallas at Irving, Texas.

1978 University of Arizona. Tucson.

1980 La Provincia en el Distrito Federal: Chiapas. Polyforum Cultura Siqueiros. Mexico City.

1982 Zur Stockeregg. Zurich, Switzerland.

1983 Casa de Cultura. Feria Internacional. Tapachula, Chiapas.

1983 Casa de Cultura. San Cristóbal de las Casas, Chiapas.

1984 International Center of Photography. New York.

Books

1944 *Los Lacandones, su pasado y su presente.* Biblioteca Enciclopédica Popular, no. 30. Secretaría de Educación Pública. Mexico City.

1946 *¿Hay razas inferiores?* Secretaría de Educación Pública. Mexico City. Republished in 1974 by Complejo Editorial Mexicano. Mexico City.

1955 *La Selva Lacandona.* 2 volumes. With Frans Blom. Editorial Libros de México. Mexico City. Photos.

1961 *Chiapas Indígenas.* Universidad Nacional Autónoma de México. Mexico City. Text and photos.

1972 *Heirs of the ancient Maya.* Text by Christine Price, photos by Gertrude Duby Blom. Scribner's. New York.

1979 *La Familia de Na Bolom.* Casa de Cultura. Monterrey, Nuevo León. Text and photos.

1982 *Das Antlitz der Mayas.* Athenäum Verlag. Königstein, Germany. Introduction and photos by Gertrude Duby Blom, text by Ossi Urchs and Sigi Höhle.

Books with Photos by Gertrude Duby Blom

1950 *Something about life in Mexico.* Pan American Union. Washington, D.C.

1974 *Cambios medicos y sociales en una comunidad Maya-Tzeltal.* Robert Harman. Instituto Nacional Indígeno. Mexico City.

1975 *Cambio cultural dirigido en los altos de Chiapas.* Ulrich Köhler. Instituto Nacional Indígeno. Mexico City.

1975 *Pursuit of the ancient Maya.* Robert Brunhouse. University of New Mexico Press. Albuquerque.

1976 *Frans Blom: Maya explorer.* Robert Brunhouse. University of New Mexico Press. Albuquerque.

1980 *Los Mayas el tiempo capturado.* Demetrio Sodi. Litógrafos Unidos. Mexico City.

1981 *The Indian Christ, the Indian king: The historical substrate of Maya myth and ritual.* Victoria Bricker. University of Texas Press. Austin.

1983 *Antropología e historia de los mixe-zoques y mayas.* Edited by Lorenzo Ochoa and Thomas Lee. UNAM and BYU. Mexico City.

1982 *The last lords of Palenque.* Robert Bruce and Victor Perera. Little, Brown. Boston.

1983 *Arte Maya: Selva y mar.* Roman Piña Chan and George Stuart. Editorial del Sureste. Mexico City.

Articles

1961 Last of the Lacandones. *Pacific Discovery.* California Academy of Sciences. 14:4. July-August. Pp. 2–11. Photos.

1965 Operation Yaxchilán. Photos. El rescate de la reina. Mexico en la Cultura. *Novedades.* 8 August.

1966 Aventura en un mundo viviente, escondido. *La Extra, El Sol de Chiapas.* 28 January.

1966 Fray Bartolomé. Mexico en la Cultura. *Novedades.* 19 June.

1966 Fray Bartolomé de las Casas: Luchador sin tregua. Introduction. Instituto de Ciencias y Artes de Chiapas. Nos. 16–17. December-January. Pp. 33–51.

1966 Pueblos en marcha: La selva reconquistada. *Circulo de Estudios Sociales.* Vol. 3, no. 1. February-April.

1966 ¿Quien es Fray Bartolomé? *Mujeres.* No. 177. Mexico City. July. P. 25.

1966 Simbólicos vitrales para la comemoración del Padre las Casas. *Excelsior.* Mexico City. 19 June.

1966 La vida de Bor Uech Yuk de Sacrum, o el fin de un gran pueblo. *Circulo de Estudios Sociales.* Escuela de Derecho de Chiapas. Vol. 3, no. 3. October-November.

1967 Desaparación de un pueblo. México en la Cultura. *Novedades.* 10, 17, 24 September. Photos.

1968 La selva Lacandona, su territorio, su gente y sus problemas. *El Nacional.* Mexico City. 4 December.

1969 The Lacandon. With Frans Blom. *Handbook of Middle American Indians.* Vol. 7, chapter 13. University of Texas Press. Austin. Pp. 276–97. Photos.

1975 Corta historia de la selva. *Excelsior.* Mexico City. 8–14 June.

1976 La selva me llama, la selva me cautiva, la selva me pide ayuda. *Excelsior.* Mexico City. 23–29 May.

1977 La selva Lacandona: ¡Reserva a futuros! *Revista Chiapas.* No. 53. September.

1977 La selva Lacandona: Una vez más nos pide a gritos, ayuda para salvar su vida. *El Día.* Mexico City. 14 May.

1977 Si queremos prosperar, cuidemos nuestra ciudad. *El Tiempo.* San Cristóbal de las Casas. 6 March.

1978 Las comunidades Indígenas, sus culturas y sus problemas de transculturación. Ponencia Reunión de Seminaria de Cultura Mexicana. 31 March–3 April.

1978 El marco de San Cristóbal de las Casas. In *Ensayos: San Cristóbal de las Casas.* Patronato Fray Bartolomé. Pp. 43–60.

1978 Miséria y atraso destruyen a la selva Lacandona. *El Gallo Ilustrado. El Día.* Mexico City. 5 March. Photos.

1979 Arrasan con la selva Lacandona. *El Sol del Campo.* 16–31 August. Photos.

1979 Continua implacable la destrucción de la selva Lacandona. *El Gallo Ilustrado. El Día.* Mexico City. 25 March. Photos.

1979 La selva Lacandona en grave riesgo. *El Dia.* Mexico City. 14 October.

1979 La selva Lacandona, reserva de la Biosfera: Una grave responsibilidad de todos. *Mujeres.* No. 343. Mexico City. July. Pp. 20–29. Photos.

1980 Los problemas de la selva Lacandona. *La Republica en Chiapas.* Tuxtla Gutiérrez. 28 February. Photos.

1980 La selva asesinada. *El Día.* Mexico City. 6 July. Photos.

1981 Esperanza perdida. *Numero Uno.* Tuxtla Gutiérrez. 26 June (3 parts). Photos.

1981 Un parque vale más para Jovel que unas cuantas oficinas. *El Tiempo.* San Cristóbal de las Casas. 21 June.

1981 El progreso no debe ser destrucción. *Numero Uno.* Tuxtla Gutiérrez. 6 October.

1982 ¿Quien destruye más, nosotros o el Chichonal? *Numero Uno.* Tuxtla Gutiérrez. 24 June. Photos.

1982 La selva Lacandona. In *Reunión Estatal para la Planeación Chiapas.* Mexico City. Pp. 165–78.

1982 Two faces of the Lacandon jungle. *The News.* Mexico City. 14 May.

1983 The death of the Lacandon culture and rainforest. *The News.* Mexico City. 18 March. Photos.